The Blessing Book

STUDY GUIDE

God's Story of Blessings
Through Eight Events

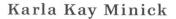

Karla Kay Minick

The following Bible translations have been used throughout *The Blessing Book Study Guide*:

(AMP) Scripture quotations from the Amplified® Bible, (AMP) Copyright © 1954, 1958, 1962, 1964, 1965, 1987 by The Lockman Foundation. Used by permission. (www.Lockman.org)

(ESV) Scripture quotations from The Holy Bible, English Standard Version®, copyright © 2001 by Crossway, a publishing ministry of Good News Publishers. Used by permission. All rights reserved.

(HCSB) Scripture quotations from the Holman Christian Standard Bible®, Copyright © 1999, 2000, 2002, 2003, 2009 by Holman Bible Publishers. Used by permission. Holman Christian Standard Bible®, Holman CSB®, and HCSB® are federally registered trademarks of Holman Bible Publishers.

(KJV) Scripture quotations from The Authorized (King James) Version. Rights in the Authorized Version in the United Kingdom are vested in the Crown. Reproduced by permission of the Crown's patentee, Cambridge University Press.

(MSG) Scripture quotations from THE MESSAGE. Copyright © by Eugene H. Peterson 1993, 1994, 1995, 1996, 2000, 2001, 2002. Used by permission of Tyndale House Publishers, Inc.

(NIV) Scripture quotations from the Holy Bible, New International Version®, NIV®. Copyright © 1973, 1978, 1984, 2011 by Biblica, Inc.TM Used by permission of Zondervan. All rights reserved worldwide. www.zondervan.com The "NIV" and "New International Version" are trademarks registered in the United States Patent and Trademark Office by Biblica, Inc.TM

(NKJV) Scripture quotations from the New King James Version®. Copyright © 1982 by Thomas Nelson. Used by permission. All rights reserved.

(NLT) Scripture quotations from the Holy Bible, New Living Translation, copyright ©1996, 2004, 2007, 2013 by Tyndale House Foundation. Used by permission of Tyndale House Publishers, Inc., Carol Stream, Illinois 60188. All rights reserved.

(TLB) Scripture quotations from The Living Bible copyright © 1971. Used by permission of Tyndale House Publishers, Inc., Carol Stream, Illinois 60188. All rights reserved.

(VOICE) Scripture quotations from The Voice™. Copyright © 2008 by Ecclesia Bible Society. Used by permission. All rights reserved.

CONTENTS

Acknowledgements   *i*

Introduction   *ii*

How to Use the Study Guide   *iii*

Desserts Over Deserts   *vi*

1 Eden: Where It All Begins   1

2 Election: Abraham's Blessing Extends to Blessing the World   7

3 Exit and Entrance: Leaving Egypt for the Promised Land   13

4 Empire: Kingdoms Established

      Part 1: The Lives of Saul and David   19

      Part 2: Solomon and the Kingdom Divided   23

5 Exile and Return: Into Captivity and Back Again   30

6 Emmanuel: God with Us through Jesus   36

7 Exhortation: Letters to Encourage and Inspire

      Part 1: The Early Church and Paul   42

      Part 2: Additional New Testament Guidance   46

8 Eternity: The Best Is yet to Come   51

Eight Memory Blessing Verses   58

Make it Yours: Memorization Tips   60

Deeper Blessings   64

Action Options   68

Acknowledgements

I'm thankful to God for the joy of learning, and I love learning more about Him as I seek to be more like Him. Growth is a process, and I thank God for His patience and encouragement as growth continues. *God, there is no one else I want to be more like than You. Thank You for adopting me and loving me so completely.*

Special thanks also to:

Russell, for the blessing of being your wife. Your faithful teaching, loving support, and consistent encouragement are an ongoing source of joy to me. God blessed me extra with you.

Three dear ladies: *Kristina,* for your first eyes on this project; you offer more than your eyes, you give your heart. *Cheryl,* for commas and building confidence for clarity; I'm grateful. *Iliana,* for your creative graphic design and inspirational insight for the layout; you are a delight to work it. I am blessed for the three of you are not only my team, but my friends. Thank you!

E and *S* thanks for the suggestion of adding recipes; journeys are sweeter when tasty treats are included!

A small team of ladies who opened up God's Word and themselves for growth to come in. Although many of you did not know each other, we gathered around my table for ten weeks as the first group to learn these blessing lessons together. Through you God's blessings continue to extend. I joyfully thank each of you.

The Blessing Book Study Guide
is dedicated to
all
who seek to journey through
God's Story of Blessings
blessing others as God has so richly blessed us.

Introduction

The Blessing Book began in 2009 when I noticed "blessing verses" during my daily reading of God's Word. It was not a book back then, just a growing list of passages jotted down in my notebook. I had hoped I would come across a book that told the blessings of God chronologically because I was intrigued and wanted to learn more. No such book crossed my path. I followed God's leading and began to write, and for that I have been blessed.

With my husband's help, we launched a site, **TheBlessingBook.com** on January 1, 2013 and interest grew. As I read responses from those I loved (and from people I did not even know) about God's blessings changing their lives, I was blessed, and I was encouraged to press through with more edits. I sought help from others to get the project into a book which can be held and read, and written in and shared. All thanks and praise to God and the team He provided; just after Thanksgiving 2014, *The Blessing Book* was first printed! Since that time it has been a joy to share the book with our neighbors, family and friends around the world and to make it available to those seeking God's goodness.

My faith increases as I read God's Story through fresh blessings each day, and I am again jotting down notes, reminders of God's present blessings in my life. It is so much fun to be a part of God's blessing cycle, and I love how we are encouraged to live life fully by seeing God's blessings in our own lives. Blessing others then becomes natural and expands God's love one person at a time.

Several readers of *The Blessing Book* daily devotional shared, "I can't stop reading after just one page, I'm days ahead!" I feel the same way. I get caught up in the beauty of God's Story, and I want to read more. Although I know how the Story ends, I don't want to wait until December 31st to get there. Inspired by Russell's teaching of the whole Old Testament in a one-day seminar, I pondered the fact that we can take in a lot of information *if* it is carefully framed. Convinced that our life can be different when we really know and then live in God's Story, I rethought the framing of *The Blessing Book*. I added more details to some of the stories, arranged it to be read chapter after chapter as well as a day by day devotional, and *The Blessing Book, Revised and Expanded* edition replaced the original the winter of 2015.

Along the way I have compiled questions, many of which I have asked myself while reading through God's Story, looking for deeper understanding. The questions throughout the Study Guide are designed to increase our over-all understanding of God's Story (which Jesus says in Luke 24 is important for understanding life) and they will be a useful tool in becoming even more aware of His blessings in our day, inspiring us to bless others out of joy.

The Study Guide divides the chronologically arranged entries of *The Blessing Book* into eight major events. This guide can be used effectively with both the original copy of *The Blessing Book* or with *The Blessing Book, Revised and Expanded* edition. The inclusion of memory verses help us to better remember the flow of God's Story so we can more easily understand centuries of history. We are all on a journey; none of us are Home yet. As sojourners we travel on with the purpose of loving God and loving people. The Study Guide will help us learn God's principles of blessings and can strengthen our ability to relate to people who have traveled before us, giving us joy and courage to live faithfully in our days. Of course, the Study Guide will lead you as an individual, but the journey's even better when small groups can meet together and learn from one another, being blessed and blessing.

As we move into God's blessings, may the Lord richly bless us with His Presence and protect us, even from ourselves, as we make the changes needed for maturity to take place. May the Lord graciously smile upon us and those we love and on those we find hard to love. May He show us His favor day by day as we extend His favor to others, and may He give to us His peace. Jesus told His followers that He offers peace like no one else can. My prayer for you is Paul's prayer for those who lived years ago in Ephesus:

I pray that God our Father and our Lord Jesus Christ will be kind to you and will bless you with peace! (Ephesians 1:2). May we experience God's blessings afresh, and with joy freshly bless others! Amen.

How to Use the Study Guide

The Blessing Book Study Guide is designed to be straightforward. Knowing and retaining God's Story helps us see its relevance for wise living in our days. In the past God blessed, and He still blesses; this encourages us to live out His blessing plan. When we belong to God, we are all on the same team desiring to better understand God's Story so our own Story can make Him smile. A good team works well together, challenging one another so that the best comes out in each individual as knowledge expands and character growth deepens.

In most conventional group studies, one leader leads and the others in the group follow. In a conventional setting, this study is helpful for **Sunday School classes, Life Bible Study groups**, and **prayer groups** that include a book from time to time, or any **growth gathering** that meets on a regular basis.

The Blessing Book Study Guide is designed to also be helpful in settings that include a **rotation of facilitators**. The ten lessons can be divided among those in the group and each meet-up time can then be led by a different person. Our unique experiences bring something new as we learn from each other. Facilitating a study that is well laid out can build confidence in living out what we are taking in. By sharing leadership responsibilities, all those who participate grow in new ways. In doing so, the cycle of blessing others by starting up new groups can naturally and joyfully go forward.

Each chapter includes a few distinct parts that build upon each other. Over the course of an hour (or the time allowed for the meeting), a leader or facilitator can chose from the specific topics below to easily involve those willing to share so the entire group can learn from each other.

Suggested Reading from *The Blessing Book*: Provide the biblical content for each major event. *A facilitator can share something from the Suggested Reading that stood out and ask a few others to do the same. This leads smoothly to:*

"What did God reveal to me, and what step will I take next?": Asking this question gives us the opportunity to reflect on the biblical content and how it relates to our present situations. *Ask something like, "In light of what we have read from this part in God's Story, what will you do differently?"*

Question to Cultivate Growth: These are questions that lead to pondering God's interaction with His children, historically and presently. *A leader can choose a few of the questions, or all of them if time allows, and ask different people to share their responses.*

The Blessing Memory Verses: These grow our awareness of the overall Story and the blessings throughout. *It is always good to reveiw the* **Blessing Memory Verses** *as a team each week. Saying the verses and the reference out loud together expands our ability for better retention.*

Paraphrasing God's Overall Story: This helps us to learn the framework of the biblical Story as we travel from one major event to the next. *Praphrasing is one of my favorite parts of learning from a group. As we hear a few people each week give their understanding of each chapter we are offered fresh perspective.*

Recording Personal Blessings: The final page of each chapter includes space and time for writing down blessings, both given and received. *Depending on the group, people may choose to share some of these blessings as praise is given back to God. This can also lead naturally to praying for people or for ways we seek to bless.*

TheBlessingBook.com provides additional helpful information and various ways for meaningful interactions. Feel free to explore the website and share what you are learning from your journey as a way of connecting with others who are also seeking to live out God's blessing plan.

The Study Guide's main biblical content comes from selected entries within *The Blessing Book*. By going to **TheBlessingBook.com**, you can find the **Suggested Reading** if you do not have a copy of *The Blessing Book*. Click on **Study Guide** and each chapter's core chronological framework is provided for you in ten selected entries. The biblical content also offers hyperlinks allowing for quick access to the full text for deeper knowledge.

Just like a memorable vacation, or a good tour, or being a part of a sports team, what often makes the adventure more meaningful is sharing it with others. Get on a team and grow together! Form a group and see how blessings can go forward! A journey through God's Story is even better when the exploration is shared.

Before we begin, may I offer a conclusion? Consider ending each meet-up time by holding hands and singing together:

"Bless God from whom all blessings flow.
Bless Him ye creatures here below.
Bless Him above ye Heavenly host.
Bless Father, Son and Holy Ghost.
Amen."

༖

Desserts Over Deserts

Maybe it is a stretch, but I like to think that Jesus would have liked fro-yo if there had been a way to freeze yogurt during His time on earth. Isaiah's prophesy foretelling Jesus says, "Look! The virgin will conceive a child! She will give birth to a son and will call him Immanuel (which means 'God is with us'). By the time this child is old enough to choose what is right and reject what is wrong, he will be eating **yogurt** and **honey**" (Isaiah 7:14b-15 NLT). Later, Matthew tells us about Jesus' cousin John living in the dessert and eating locusts and honey. When given a choice, I would choose desserts over deserts and yogurt over locusts, but with Jesus we can have gratitude for all that life holds.

Desserts are a great way to sweeten up a gathering. To help make it easy to decide on what to make, here are a few tried and true recipes chosen for their yum-factor and for how easy it is to make them. Only one of the recipes requires a mixer; most can be made from one bowl, and all of them are sure to please someone. None are low-carb, low-sugar or low-taste, but at least one is gluten-free. My theory on desserts: full flavor with moderation on serving size is better than eating a lot of something that does not really satisfy. If we were making up desserts together, you would not only get a dessert but a little backstory about each particular tasty delight, so guess what? Stories included; wish we were in the kitchen together!

༄

Blond Brownies
(oldie and goldie)

My mom is my inspiration for baking up good things that bring family and people at all kinds of gatherings closer together. So the first recipe I will share is in her honor. Mom, once a Michigan farm girl, was 17 when she was introduced to Blond Brownies and they were the first thing that I remember her teaching me to bake. Everyone loves them, and why not, they hold all the yum of a chocolate chip cookie but take far less time to make. I have not tweaked this recipe but pass it on to you the way she gave it to me, including no need for the "e" after blond.

Preheat oven to 350°F
In a medium bowl add:
- **1/2 cup shortening** *(I use Crisco butter flavor)**
- **1 1/2 cup brown sugar**
- **2 eggs**
- **1 teaspoon vanilla** *(I use McCormick Vanilla, Butter & Nut Flavor)**

Mix the above together and then add:
- **1 1/4 cup flour**
- **1 1/2 teaspoons baking powder,** mix together and then mix in:
- **1/2 cup chopped walnuts**
- **6 ounces of chocolate chips** *(I use dark chocolate chips)**

Put into a greased and floured 9X13 cake pan.
Bake at 350°F for 20 minutes until light brown. Store in an airtight container and they do freeze well too.

*I means my mom. Mom has been blessing family, friends, neighbors, and even strangers with this yummy dessert since 1958.

Rice Krispie Treats
(quick and nostalgic)

Always a yummy choice! You would think that in Asia (the land of rice) it would be easy to get crispy rice cereal, right? Well, back in the day it was not. It became a tradition for me to hunt down the needed ingredients and make these special treats for Hannah, Sophie, Isaiah (and their friends) in celebration of the last day of school for each year they studied at Grace International School in Thailand.

Basically you need 3 ingredients and about 15 minutes. But before you mix it up, prepare a 9X13 inch pan by greasing it with butter. Okay, now turn the stovetop to low heat and get started.

In a large sauce pan, melt:
- **1/2 stick butter** and add:
- **10.5 ounces of miniature marshmallows** (a normal sized bag) and using a long wooden spoon stir until they are melted.

Bonus: Sometimes I add 1 teaspoon of vanilla. Sometimes I add 1 heaping tablespoon of peanut butter.

Remove from heat and quickly stir in:
- **1 13 ounce box of Rice Krispie Cereal** (about 8.5 cups)

Pat this firmly into your baking pan and if it is sticky, put a little butter on your fingers and press on to completion. Actually, it is always sticky, so before patting, put a little butter on your fingers. Cut into squares when completely cooled and store in an airtight container.

Tip: it is best not to double this recipe as getting all the cereal to mix quickly can be a challenge, so make two normal size batches if you need a lot of these treats.

Extras: add a little fun flair by strategically placing candy pieces. Estimate where you will cut the bars then place a candy in each "square". I have used gummy bears, gum drops, m&m's, and candy corn. Just be sure to press the candy firmly while the marshmallows are still warm. If you really need to be sure the candy is not going anywhere, wait until the treats have cooled, then cut into squares, then make up frosting (or buy it) and squeeze a small dollop on each square and secure the candy in place.

Energy Bars
(my all-time most asked for dessert)

When we first moved to China butter was hard to come by. How blessed I was when Beth, a friend and partner in ministry, shared with us this yummy recipe that used oil instead of butter. It started out as cookies; over the years I have done some tweaking, keeping all the yum but reducing some of the effort.

Preheat oven to 350°F
In large bowl, mix:
- **1 1/4 cup oatmeal** (put in first as this makes them healthy)
- **2/3 cup brown sugar**
- **1/2 cup white sugar**
- **1 cup flour**
- **1/2 teaspoon each of salt, baking soda, and baking powder**
- **1 cup chocolate chips**

OR

1 cup of m&m's, white chocolate chips, peanut butter chips, diced apples with cinnamon, nuts, craisins, raisins… you get the idea. Just be sure your add-ins equal about 1 cup total.

Then mix in a pyrex measuring cup:
- **1/2 cup oil**
- **1 egg**
- **1 teaspoon vanilla**

Add to the dry mixture and give it all a good stir until well combined.

Pat the dough into a greased 9x13 inch baking pan and bake at 350°F for about 10-12 minutes. Place on a cooling rack. Cut while warm but serve when completely cooled. Bring on the yum! This recipe doubles very nicely if you need to offer lots and lots of energy.

Something fun to do: in the autumn buy several large bags of m&m's. Divide out the colors...all the brown, orange and yellow ones put in a zip-lock bag and use to make Energy Bars at Thanksgiving. All the red and green ones bag up and save for Christmas Energy Bars. The blue m&m's are left... if you do not need to make a dessert for a baby boy shower then you get to eat all the blue ones...more energy for you!

Lemon Bars

(Franny's favorite)

I did not know that by marrying Russell I would also be blessed with his mom's wonderful Lemon Bars; another great perk in our marriage! These are not really quick or easy to make, and they are loaded with sugar, but every now and then they are just what is needed, especially when life gives us lemons!

Preheat oven to 350°F
Put waxed paper in a 9X13 inch pan leaving some paper to drape over all the edges.
In a medium bowl make the crust:
- **1 cup butter**
- **2 cups flour**
- **1/2 cup powdered sugar**

Mix with a fork or a pastry cutter, like you are making a pie crust and pat into the prepared pan. Bake 17-ish minutes and let cool on a rack. While the crust is baking and cooling prepare the filling by whisking the following together until smooth in the same bowl you used for making the crust:
- **4 eggs**
- **2 cups sugar**
- **8 tablespoons lemon juice (about 1/2 cup)**
- **4 tablespoons flour**
- **1 teaspoon baking powder**
- **Pinch of salt**

(Sometimes I add a little yellow food color just for fun.)

Zest of 1 lemon *is not in Franny's recipe but it really is a good addition. And if you really like things zesty you can also add some lemon zest to the crust before baking it. ("Zesting" the lemon before squeezing it works best; just another little thing I have learned from experience.)*

Pour this mixture over the cooled crust and re-bake it all for an additional 17-ish minutes. When you give the pan a little shake in the oven, the middle should be solid, not jiggly.

Tip on how to more easily cut lemon bars:
Place them from the oven to the freezer to cool. When chilled remove from the pan by gently lifting with the waxed paper edges and then put them flat on a large cutting board, pealing down the waxed paper. Cut with a rolling pizza cutter and place on a serving plate.

Topping:
Sprinkle with powdered sugar. To keep this from clumping up, I put the powder sugar in a small sieve or a sifter and sprinkle. These can be stored in an airtight container (with waxed paper separating the layers) and also frozen.

I thank God for the many good memories of Franny in our lives. May this Lemon Bar recipe bless you and those you love too.

No-Bakes

(oven not required)

Hey, don't have an oven but still hungry for cookies? Don't settle for store-bought, make these yummy No-Bakes instead. The gals at the Thai juvenile detention center really liked this treat. While making them together in their oven-free, open-air kitchen, I was able to share how the Bible is like a recipe… "If we follow God's plan our lives are so much sweeter!" One gal piped up, "Yeah, yeah…let's make the cookies!"

Here goes:
Place enough waxed paper for 24 spoonfuls (or 2 dozen cup-cake papers), on the counter. Separately, measure out:
- **1/2 cup peanut butter**
- **2 1/2 cups oatmeal**

Then in a medium-size sauce pan (we used a wok in the prison), add:
- **2 cups sugar**

- **1/2 cup milk**
- **1/2 teaspoon salt**
- **3 tablespoon cocoa**

Mix this together with a long wooden spoon, then turn on the heat to medium high. Bring to a boil. When it starts to bubble, cook about 1 1/2 minutes more, stirring constantly. (Do not over-cook!… if that sounds too bossy, "it is best if you do not over-cook".)

Remove from heat and quickly add:
- **1/2 cup peanut butter**
- **2 teaspoons vanilla** and mix until smooth, then mix in the **2 1/2 cups oatmeal** that you have pre-measured.

Then quickly spoon into paper cups or onto waxed paper. Let cool and enjoy! Yield: 2 dozen cookies. Store in an airtight container.

If you do over cook the No-Bakes, don't throw them away but put the crumbled mixture in an airtight container and use for a yummy ice cream or frozen yogurt topping. Redemption is always God's best.

Frozen Yogurt

(the Isaiah 7:15 dessert?)

There are lots of make-at-home frozen yogurt recipes out there. Since I presently work at a frozen yogurt shop, I have not tried any of the recipes, but at various times I've purchased the ingredients only to later use them in different ways. My best recommendation is to go to Menchie's, or the fro-yo place near to you and choose a few different flavors (Takes the Cake Batter is our number one seller) and put them in your freezer until you are ready to serve it up. After it is frozen it will scoop right out like ice cream. While in the yogurt shop, peruse the snack-age area for ideas, then head to Kroger (after the fro-yo is safe in your freezer), and pick up a few of the items that caught your eye for toppings. Having a variety of toppings from healthy to decadent makes it a fun dessert for everyone. Picking up a quart of sorbet blesses those who are lactose intolerant and sweet conversations are sure to follow.

Some might choose to over-cook the No-Bakes recipe just to have a tasty homemade topping to add to the mix. Be sure to have honey on hand; that is the way Jesus ate His yogurt.

Sweet and Salty Chex Mix

(loved it but have not made it)

I have not tried this recipe on my own yet as it makes a ton so I need to save it for a holiday or for a big group study session! Nearly 20 years after sharing life in a Newly Married class in Dallas, five soul sisters reconnected in Arkansas and shared this great snack. I love that when you stay close to God, the sweet (laughter and gladness) can intermingle with the salty (tears of deep sadness) and the result grows us to worship God and to bless those He blesses us to journey alongside.

What you need:
- **3 sticks butter**
- **2 cups brown sugar**
- **1 cup karo syrup**
- **2 teaspoons vanilla**
- **1 teaspoon baking soda**
- **1/3 of one bag of pretzels** (I would use the thin stick kind)
- **1 can (16 oz.) cocktail peanuts**
- **1 box Rice Chex**
- **1 box Wheat Chex**

Also have handy 1 brown paper grocery bag (coat inside with baking spray) and about 6 cookie sheets lined with foil and sprayed with baking spray.

How to make:

Mix 1/2 of both cereals, 1/2 of the peanuts, and 1/2 of the pretzels in the sprayed paper bag. In a medium sauce pan bring the butter, brown sugar, and karo syrup to a boil, stirring all the while. Boil for 5 minutes. Remove from heat. Add vanilla then the baking soda and mix well. Pour 1/2 of the hot sugar-butter mixture on top of the cereal combination in the bag. Shake it a bit. Add the rest of the the cereal, nuts, pretzels and top with the remaining hot sugar-butter mixture. Using two wooden spoons mix and turn as best you can. Fold/roll down the bag and microwave for 1 minute. Stir. Repeat 3 times. Cool the *Sweet and Salty Chex Mix* by spreading it out on the prepared cookie sheets and then store in airtight containers. You need to give it a good shake every now and then to keep it from sticking together.

This recipe certainly makes enough to bless many. In the sweet times, in the salty times, let's bless on!

Peanut Butter Cookies

(gluten-free 3 ingredient yum!)

3 ingredient peanut butter cookies are so easy and gluten-free, way before I even knew that the term "gluten-free" existed. I first made these great tasting cookies back in high school and still enjoy baking them up today. Before going forward, it might be good to make sure you have milk on hand. Why? Because I think these cookies are best enjoyed with milk.

Preheat oven to 350°F

So the three ingredients are... (can you guess?)
- **1 egg**
- **1 cup sugar**
- **1 cup peanut butter** (this will make about 1 dozen cookies)

The way I like to make them is to double the recipe. Buy a normal size jar of peanut butter which is about 16 ounces (I like to use the smooth). With a rubber spatula remove all the peanut butter and put it in a bowl. Now fill the jar up again with sugar, leave a little room so you can give it a good shake (helping to remove any of the remaining peanut butter) and add it to the bowl. Crack 2 eggs into the again empty peanut butter jar, put the lid back on and shake it until the eggs become well-beaten and then pour them also in the bowl. Stir the three ingredients until well blended. Egg size varies so if the batter is too sticky to roll into balls, put it in the refrigerator for a little while. Roll into balls. Dip the balls in a little bowl of sugar, then press down on the balls, one at a time, criss-crossing them with a fork. Bake about 8 minutes at 350°F, cool on racks, and everyone is ready to enjoy the treat!

It is also fun to carefully wash out the peanut butter jar, dry it, and use it to deliver 6 or 7 of the cookies to new neighbors with the recipe attached as a "welcome to the neighborhood gift".

Cinnamon Wraps

(need only one little bowl and a sharp knife)

The ladies in my Life Bible Study Group aka: Sunday School Class, were having a bring-a-dish-to-share breakfast before our study. It was about 20 minutes before our etd (estimate time of departure) for church when I remembered saying I would bring something for the breakfast. Hmmmm. *The night before we ate a Mexican dinner at Lupe's Tortillas (some of the best flour tortillas in the world and a bonus for living in Texas). Lupe's is generous with their tortillas and so I had some wrapped up in the fridge leftover from our meal. You can probably guess where this is going...*

What to do:
Preheat oven to 350°F
Place wax paper on a cookie sheet.
In a small bowl combine 3 parts sugar to one part cinnamon.

This combination stores nicely, so to make it easy, mix:
- **3/4 cup sugar and**
- **1/4 cup cinnamon** (The best cinnamon I have ever had was from a super cool open-air market in Vietnam. I still had some left from when we had meetings in Vietnam, so I splurged and used it.)

Spread room-temperature **butter** on the **flour tortilla**. Sprinkle generously with the cinnamon-sugar. Roll it up. Cut into 1 inch slices. Place on cookie sheet the way you would cinnamon rolls. Repeat until all your tortillas are gone. Bake until the cinnamon gets a little bubbly, this will not take long, so do not leave the kitchen but check the progress at about 5 minutes. Arrange on serving platter and cover (I use un-used shower caps, as they stretch nicely over dinner plates and keep everything in place) and now you are ready to go!

I have tried the Cinnamon Wraps again with store-bought flour tortillas; it works, but of course the yum-factor is way higher with Lupe's!

Yogurt Apple Bars
(3 bowls: 2 smalls and 1 large)

Yogurt Apple Bars were created one morning when I was making up normal apple bars, but late into the game I found out I did not have an egg. So began my dilemma. Do I get dressed and bike to the Kroger, or maybe run to the Kroger instead as I wanted to fit a run in and eggs aren't that heavy to run with. Or do I borrow an egg from a neighbor, if so which one, and I would still need to get dressed... The oven had already preheated; I wanted to get the bars baking and get back to my edits. Arrangements were in place with Kristina to visit Julianna who had just had a baby (that was who I was baking for). I needed a fast plan to move forward, what was a girl to do? Then I remembered "substitutions" so I quickly went online, found a variety of egg substitutions and chose to use yogurt because I had bought some the night before (why didn't I remember to buy eggs?). The yogurt was pumpkin spice and it went great with green apple that was already prepared for the apple bars. So here we have it, to celebrate Julianna's second son: the birth of another fine recipe!

Preheat oven to 350°F
In a small bowl mix:
- **1/2 cup brown sugar**
- **1/2 cup white sugar**
- **1 apple, diced** (I keep the peelings on and this time used a green apple)
- **1 tablespoon cinnamon**

Mix this first so the apple gets nice and covered with the cinnamon and can "juice-up" a little.

In a large bowl, mix:
- **1 cup flour with**
- **1 1/2 cup oatmeal**
- **1/2 teaspoon each of salt, baking soda, and baking powder**

In a separate small bowl mix:
- **1 1/2 cup oil with**
- **1 teaspoon vanilla and**
- **1/4 cup yogurt** (Oh, and if you do not have yogurt, use 1 egg.)

Mix this into the large flour bowl and then combine the apple mixture until well mixed. Spray pans with baking spray before baking at 350°F for about 20 minutes. As I was giving these to two different friends, I used two 7X7 inch disposable aluminum pans that you buy with the clear plastic lids included. But it can be baked all together in one 9x13 inch size pan. When the apple bars are cooling, drizzle on a little caramel sauce if you want to make it extra yummy. Cut before serving. These freeze really nicely too.

Coconut Cookies

(3 ingredients—need a mixer)

Back in 2006, Germany Mary came to Thailand to live with our family and learn to speak English. While she was with us we learned a lot from her too. One thing was how to make coconut cookies. Although I really do not care for coconut, somehow I like these cookies.

Preheat oven to 300°F

Here's how to make them in US language and measurements.

Begin with:

- **3 egg whites**…the easiest way I have found to separate egg whites from the yolk is to carefully crack the egg in half then slowly move the yolk from one shell to the other allowing the white to drip into the bowl you are going to be using…in this case, a large-size mixing bowl. (Save the three yolks to add to scrambled eggs for your next breakfast.)

Now add:

- **3 pinches of salt** (if you prefer more exact measurements, 3 of my pinches equals 1/8 teaspoon)

Beat the egg whites and salt with an electric mixer on medium until soft peaks begin to form, about 3 minutes.

Now add:

- **1 cup sugar** slowly until it's all blended in. Now you can kick it up to high speed on your mixer and continue mixing for an additional 3 minutes. This is so white and beautifully clean, like fresh Michigan snow, but without the need of mittens, boots or a box of Kleenex!

Using a spoon, mix in:

- **1 1/2 cup sweetened coconut flakes**

A tablespoon works nicely to drop the cookie mixture (it will have the consistency of meringue) onto waxed paper on cookie sheets and bake for about 20 minutes until they are just barely turning off-white. Place the cookie sheet on a rack and let cool completely, then remove them to a serving plate. These cookies have a sweet and wholesome taste and a bit of a nice crunch. Yield: 2 1/2 to 3 dozen, depending on the size.

*Thank you Mary for sharing your recipe with us! These are **sehr gut**!*

Chocolate Brownies

(as my British friend would say, "easy-peasy-lemon-squeezy")

Each Christmas season the ladies who minister weekly to the gals at the Thai juvenile center plan a big celebration. Husbands and children of the team join in with the young ladies and their guards bringing a family atmosphere of fun and hope. That means we need lots of brownies. Bronwen, our fearless leader, provided what I think might be the world's easiest chocolate brownie recipe and it is really good, too.

Preheat oven to 350°F
In a large pyrex bowl, microwave:

- **1 cup of butter** 30 seconds or until it melts

add:

- **1 cup cocoa powder**
- **2 cups sugar**
- **3 eggs**
- **1 teaspoon vanilla**

With a spoon, mix just enough to combine the ingredients.
then add:

- **1 cup of flour,** mix in but do not over-mix

Spray baking spray into a 9x13 inch pan, spoon in the batter. Before baking it is optional to sprinkle with sprinkles, chocolate chips, or nuts. (Actually, if you add nuts, mix them in.) Or top with a light layer of powdered sugar after the brownies have baked and cooled.

Bake at 350°F for 29-ish minutes. Do the toothpick test so you do not over-bake these. Cool on a rack and cut into squares while a little bit warm. Store in an airtight container.

And a bonus recipe:

6-Chocolate Chocolate Brownies

(a little more extensive, but oh so worth it!)

Over time I have tweaked Bronwen's recipe for easy chocolate brownies. The last time I made the brownies (for a group celebrating Russell's good teaching of Jesus' great sermon on the mount) may have been the best yet.

Here's what I did:
Preheat oven to 350°F

- **1/2 cup butter** (This is one stick, as that was all I had, and I like the salted option.) in a 2-cup pyrex measuring cup microwave until melted, about 30 seconds.

add:

- **1 teaspoon vanilla**
- **1/4 cup canola oil**
- **1/4 cup olive oil**

(This is now the equivalent of 1 cup of butter, but a little more healthy.)

Pour this into a large mixing bowl.

- **3 eggs** into the pyrex measuring cup and stir until mixed, pour into the bowl

Measure:

- **1/2 cup cold coffee** (leftover from breakfast) into the measuring cup and then pour into the bowl (this helps get any remaining oil or egg out of the measuring cup, for easier clean up). The coffee is useful now instead of going down the sink and brings out great richness in the brownies.
- **1 cup cocoa powder** I chose three different darknesses (1/3 cup of each).

Add:

- **2 cups sugar**

Mix this with a spoon just long enough to combine.

Lastly add:

- **1 cup flour**
- **1 handful of dark chocolate chips** (My handful equals about 1/2 cup, if your hands are bigger, then that means a little more chocolate!)
- **1 handful of white chocolate chips**
- **1/2 handful of organic raw cocoa nibs** (I bought these in hopes of helping with my migraine; they did not, but now they sure make some happy chocolate brownies.)

Mix with a spoon again just enough to combine; do not over-mix. Spray a 9X13 inch baking pan with baking spray. Spoon the batter into the pan, sprinkle a few more of the dark chocolate chips, white chocolate chips and organic raw cacao nibs on top. Bake at 350° F for 29-ish minutes. Do the toothpick test so you do not over-bake it. Cool on a rack. Cut while a little bit warm. Store in an airtight container, but there will probably not be left-overs.

❧

I hope that these recipes are a help and an inspiration to make your Blessing Book Study times even sweeter for your group. By rotating who provides the snack, all can get involved and again share in the joy of the journey. Having snack-sized zip-lock bags on hand can spread the goodness further when it is time to say Good-Bye. Feel free to visit **MinickMenus.blogspot.com** *for photos of these recipes and a host of other tried and true options. There is always something good someone is sharing with me, and I love passing on the blessing!*

Enjoy!

1

Eden

WHERE IT ALL BEGINS

◆ ‣ TIME FRAME: THE BEGINNING ‣ ◆

This first chapter marks the spot for God's Story of blessings to begin. Our starting point is a beautiful garden many years ago. As we establish our bearings, let's gather the equipment needed for the journey. Along with *The Blessing Book* (or the **Suggested Reading** content found online) and this Study Guide, it is helpful to have your own copy of the Bible for highlighting the new things we will learn. Also, a dozen or so note cards will be handy from the start, and I will tell you more about these later in a few pages. Maybe the most important thing we need for the quest before us is a prayerful heart and mind, one that prepares us to receive and give blessings.

Our Father,
we are excited for the journey before us.
Thank You for blessing us by creating us in Your image.
Please open our eyes, minds and hearts up to You
and how we can be actively involved in Your blessing plan.
Amen.

🌿

Suggested Reading from *The Blessing Book:*

🌿 JANUARY 1   Blessed to Sing God's Praises Like the Birds

🌿 JANUARY 2   Made in God's Image and Blessed!*

🌿 JANUARY 3   Blessed to Rest

🌿 JANUARY 4   Blessing upon Blessing

🌿 JANUARY 5   Bless the Lord All My Days

🌿 JANUARY 6   Blessed to Start Again

🌿 JANUARY 7   Blessed to Be Fruitful

🌿 JANUARY 8   Blessed Be the Lord

*This entry contains the memory blessing verse for Eden: Where It All Begins.

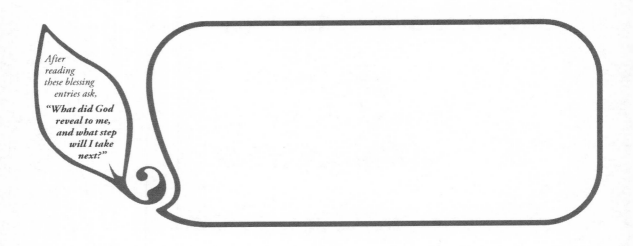

After reading these blessing entries ask,

"What did God reveal to me, and what step will I take next?"

Questions to cultivate growth:

The opening eleven chapters of Genesis introduces us to God's Story, and we see God's love and blessings from the very beginning. We've just read *The Blessing Book's* first eight entries, and we notice how Jesus is involved with creation (John 1), and we see how the psalmist blesses God for creating a world filled with goodness (Psalm 104).

1. In the order of their appearance, here are the first few characters we meet on our journey. They, like all of us, are presented with choices. Jot down what you can learn from the choices of:

   ETERNAL ONE:

   ADAM:

   EVE:

   SERPENT:

   CAIN:

   ABEL:

   Several generations later...
   NOAH:

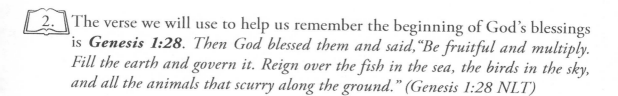

2. The verse we will use to help us remember the beginning of God's blessings is *Genesis 1:28*. *Then God blessed them and said, "Be fruitful and multiply. Fill the earth and govern it. Reign over the fish in the sea, the birds in the sky, and all the animals that scurry along the ground." (Genesis 1:28 NLT)*

   Read Genesis 1 in your Bible, and when you come to *Genesis 1:28*, highlight the word "blessed."

3. Picture the setting of the verse as you read Genesis 1:28. What stands out as interesting? Who is doing the talking in Genesis 1:28 and who is the audience? What do we learn about God's character from this verse?

4. We see that mankind is blessed by God, and from that blessing we are then given a responsibility. How does this initial "blessed before action" concept make you feel?

5. Capture the essence of Chapter 1, Eden: Where It All Begins. Summarize the content of the time frame from Creation up through Noah in one to three sentences. **Here is an example:** *In the beginning God created all things good. He blessed humanity and trusted them to care for creation, but it does not go well. Yet God's plan of blessings will not be undermined— blessings will go forth; original blessing came before original sin.*

*Paraphrase Chapter 1, **Eden:** Where It All Begins.*

To enhance our journey please read through the **Eight Memory Blessing Verses** at the back of this book on page 58. These verses are our road map through the events in God's Story. Jesus says in Luke 24 that we are to know God's Story, so we can make sense of the circumstances in our own lives. Write the eight memory blessing verses onto note cards. Over the course of the study, we will seek to memorize them, really taking them to heart. Don't let this overwhelm you, but view it as an opportunity for great growth. For now let's just get acquainted with the memory verses and begin to ponder Genesis 1:28.

For helpful guidance to increase your skill at memorizing Bible verses, please see **Make It Yours: Memorization Tips**. These principles will help us with our eight memory blessing verses. The tips are on page 60.

Page 64 offers some suggestions called **Deeper Blessings**—ideas that can deepen our understanding of God's plan of blessings, which grows our love. These suggestions can be considered after each chapter or later, perhaps as an additional personal study. Deeper Blessings are purely optional for your benefit as they fit into your days. One way to become more intentional in cultivating character growth is to implement the discipline of recording our blessings. **Ideas for Using a Blessing Journal** are at the end of the Deeper Blessings section to inspire and give some helpful tips. For this study the final page of each chapter is designed to be used as a Blessing Journal. As we realize our blessings and are thankful to God for them, our usefulness and our joy in blessing others increases.

One last tool to introduce as we embark on the journey of blessings before us is some practical applications starters called **Action Options**. These can be found in a list starting on page 68. Action Options (each beginning with a verb) help us to connect our minds with our bodies as we explore a principle and turn it to action in order to better engage with God and with others on our journey.

I hope that Chapter 1 has been a wonderful starting point, giving us not only the specifics of the beginning of blessings as experienced in the event of Eden, but also a brief overview of the adventure before us. We all come into a dedicated time of study with different goals, expectations, and prior commitments on our time. It is almost certain that unexpected challenges will come up which may hinder at times our ability to complete our lessons. Please still join the weekly meet up sessions because God can use us to bless each other in many ways as we journey on together, learning from Him as our Faithful Guide. One of the blessings and joys of a small group study is that it includes time to get to know others on the journey. Let's not miss out on the opportunity to be blessed and to bless!

God allows us to give and receive blessings of all sizes. To grow our awareness of His blessing plan, think over a few of the blessings you have experienced this week. *God, I thank You for these gifts:*

2

Election

ABRAHAM'S BLESSING EXTENDS TO BLESSING THE WORLD

TIME FRAME: APPROXIMATELY 2100 BC—1500BC

In this chapter we learn God's specific blessing promise which begins with God choosing or electing Abraham so that through Abraham, the whole world is blessed. Blessing all of humanity is a dominate theme throughout God's Story. God's blessing gets passed on from generation to generation and as we read about the patriarchs, we also learn about their different personalities. Chapter 2 has 36 entries from January 9 to February 13. The following ten entries provide you with the core chronological framework for Abraham's story through to Jacob and his sons.

Thank You Father
for Your promise of blessing that extends to all people in all places.
Help us to be a part of passing on Your goodness to those in our generation.
Grow our awareness of Your grace and blessings
so our love for You deepens and joy overflows.
Amen.

❦

Suggested Reading from *The Blessing Book:*

- 🍃 JANUARY 9   We Are Blessed to Bless *
- 🍃 JANUARY 12   Blessed to Change
- 🍃 JANUARY 15   Blessed to Pass the Test
- 🍃 JANUARY 20   Blessed Future
- 🍃 JANUARY 22   God's Blessing Passed Down
- 🍃 JANUARY 26   Blessing of Heaven's Dew and Earth's Richness
- 🍃 FEBRUARY 1   Asher—Blessed to Be Happy
- 🍃 FEBRUARY 5   The Blessing of Forgiveness
- 🍃 FEBRUARY 7   Blessed for the Sake of Another
- 🍃 FEBRUARY 9   End of Life Blessings

*This entry contains the memory blessing verse for Election: Abraham's Blessing Extends to Blessing the World.

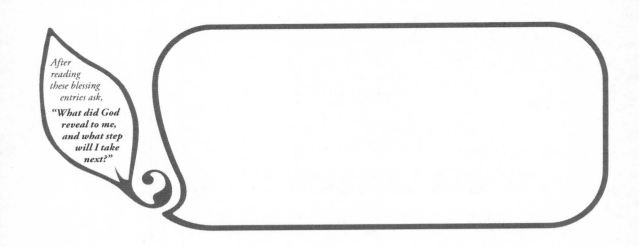

After reading these blessing entries ask,

"What did God reveal to me, and what step will I take next?"

Questions to cultivate growth:

1. Prayerfully read **Genesis 12** in your Bible and highlight the "bless" words at the beginning in verses 2–3.

2. Here is **Genesis 12:2–3 NIV** again as it is the key passage to the blessings that follow in God's Story. The blessing is contingent on Abraham leaving behind what was familiar to him.

   "I will make you into a great nation, and I will bless you; (Abram was still childless when God addressed him.) *I will make your name great, and you will be a blessing.* (God even changed Abram's name.) *I will bless those who bless you, and whoever curses you I will curse;* (God is for Abraham and his friends and is against Abe's enemies.) *and all peoples on earth will be blessed through you."* (We are all blessed through this promise given to Abraham.)

   As you begin to put Genesis 12:2–3 to memory, think about the implications of this passage in your own life, thanking God for the blessings He gives.

   Who has shared with you the blessing of knowing God?

   Both words and actions teach us more of who God is, and we long for not just a one-time encounter but a life-time relationship.

   In what ways are you passing on the blessing?

Abraham's Family Tree

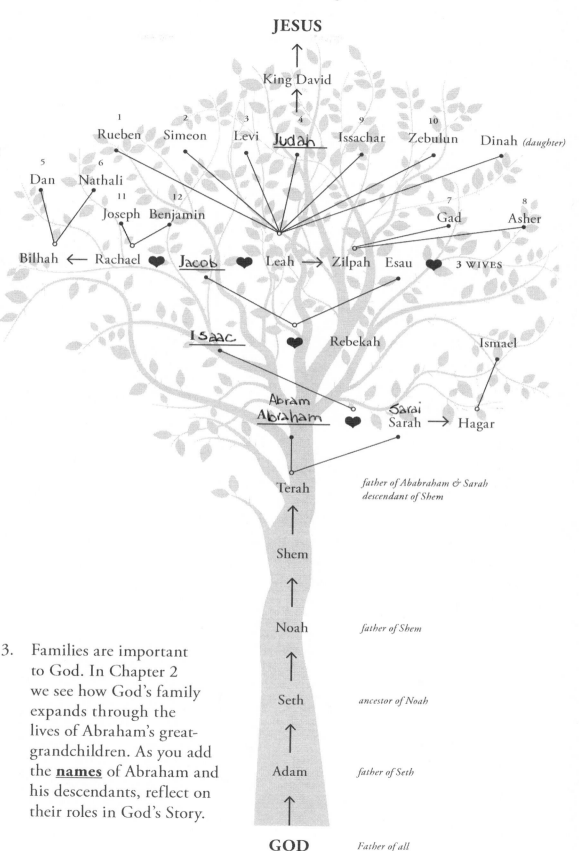

JESUS

King David

1 Rueben 2 Simeon 3 Levi 4 **Judah** 9 Issachar 10 Zebulun Dinah *(daughter)*

5 Dan 6 Nathali

11 Joseph 12 Benjamin

7 Gad 8 Asher

Bilhah ← Rachael ❤ **Jacob** ❤ Leah → Zilpah Esau ❤ 3 WIVES

Isaac ❤ Rebekah Ismael

Abram
Abraham ❤ Sarai
Sarah → Hagar

Terah *father of Ababraham & Sarah*
descendant of Shem

Shem

Noah *father of Shem*

3. Families are important to God. In Chapter 2 we see how God's family expands through the lives of Abraham's great-grandchildren. As you add the **names** of Abraham and his descendants, reflect on their roles in God's Story.

Seth *ancestor of Noah*

Adam *father of Seth*

GOD *Father of all*

4. Where are you in the family tree? Jesus will later say that whoever does God's will becomes His family members. We all love belonging and being blessed. In a way that is meaningful, seek to bless a particular person in your family in a specific way this week. Write down their name here and on your Blessing Journal page at the end of this chapter. _____

Paraphrase Chapter 2, **Election:** *Abraham's Blessing Extends to Blessing the World*

5. Practice saying your paraphrased version of Chapter 1 and connect it to Chapter 2. It might help to think about just the historical highlights of these times. Include main characters as well as God's involvement in His Story as you practice your paraphrase. Hearing your own words out loud can help you remember the Story even better.

6. Review your **Memory Blessing Verses**. First mankind was blessed by God, (Genesis 1:28) and now one man, Abraham, is blessed so that everyone else will know God's blessings (Genesis 12:2–3). Abraham's family did expand and became so big that we will read how the Israelites become a threat in the eyes of the Egyptians. Suspension builds. Write out our first two memory verses.

GENESIS 1:28 NLT:

GENESIS 12:2–3 NIV:

Understand

Remember

Use

When I was in the Marine Corps, we used a lot of acronyms, and some of them really helped me remember important things. The acronym **URU** can help us as we go forward in our study of God's Word through blessings. Our goal is:

Deeper **understanding** can come with interactive exposure to information. We can then **remember** this information—in this study it is primarily God's Story—by intentionally focusing on it and retelling it in our own words. We **use** what we learn and experience by receiving blessings and by blessing others.

URU reminds us that we are unique and the way we take in and live out God's blessings will be different for each of us. When we encounter people (past or present) that appear to have aspects of godly character that we desire, it is easy to become jealous. We are all on a journey and Christ-likeness is a process. Rather than obsessing on comparisons, let's thank God for the uniqueness within His children and seek to learn from people He places in our lives. We all have a role in God's Story. Before we prepare for the exhilarating and physically demanding rescue mission of Chapter 3, let's take some time to reflect on our most recent blessings.

We focused on Abraham and his extended family this week. How has God used you to bless your family? In what ways has your family blessed you? *Prayerfully record a few of your blessings:*

3

Exit and Entrance

LEAVING EGYPT FOR THE PROMISED LAND

TIME FRAME: APPROXIMATELY 1500 BC

Moses is God's right-hand man for more than half of Chapter 3. His involvement with God's Story is movie worthy, to say the least. Joshua enters the Story as the Promised Land is divided. Then we'll meet a few judges and conclude the chapter with the love story of Ruth. Chapter 3 has 53 entries from February 14 to April 6. The following ten entries provide you with the core chronological framework for the story of Moses and the miraculous exit from Egypt through the entrance to the Promised Land.

God,
we see miracles lived out in Moses' lifetime
and as we reflect on these blessings, we know You are powerful.
These signs and wonders point to Your perfect provision in Jesus.
Let us hold fast to Him as the Rescuer who You have provided for our lives,
for our souls.
Amen.

Suggested Reading from *The Blessing Book:*

FEBRUARY 14 A Hard Heart toward God's Blessing

FEBRUARY 16 Blessed by God Who Delivers *

FEBRUARY 21 Painful Blessing of Loyalty

MARCH 8 Blessed to Be Joyful, Thankful, and Prayerful

MARCH 13 Blessed Not to Be Greedy

MARCH 17 Stubborn Hearts Will Not Be Blessed

MARCH 22 Blessed to Carry and Pass the Baton of Faith

MARCH 24 Some Blessings Need to Be Asked For

MARCH 28 Blessed among Tent-Dwelling Women

APRIL 1 From Bitter to Better to Blessed

*This entry contains the memory blessing verse for Exit and Entrance: Leaving Egypt for the Promised Land.

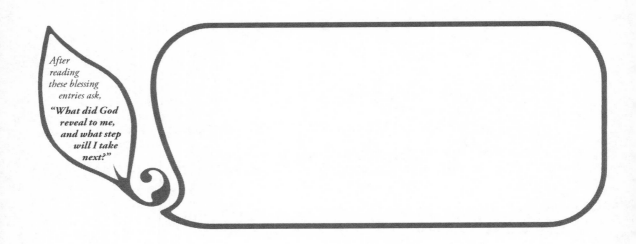

After
reading
these blessing
entries ask,

**"What did God
reveal to me,
and what step
will I take
next?"**

Questions to cultivate growth:

1. Moses lived a long life spanning three distinct 40-year periods. Briefly describe his life in each of the three stages, remembering that God does not waste experiences but can redeem them. Be sure to include details like where he was living, what his major roles were, and who he was close to in each stage of life. Get creative in your thinking, trying to really picture what his life was like.

    STAGE 1:

    STAGE 2:

    STAGE 3:

2. Whatever your age is now, divide your life into three segments. Draw out a bit about each of these stages. If the location you were living and your various roles help you distinguish your distinct stages, be sure to include them. Did you feel particularly close to God in a certain season? Try to remember why. How has God blessed you in each of these stages so far, and what were ways you have been a blessing to Him and to others? What hopes do you have for the next stage of your life?

STAGE 1:

STAGE 2:

STAGE 3:

NEXT STAGE:

3. We met many interesting people as we traveled through Chapter 3. We can learn from both positive and negative examples, so jot down a few things that stand out to you from those listed below. Which character traits would you like to model?

MOSES:

AARON:

PHARAOH (and the Egyptians):

JETHRO:

JOSHUA:

CALEB:

JAEL:

RUTH (and family):

4. Read *Exodus 18* in your Bible and highlight "blessed" in verse ten. Moses shared with Jethro the goodness of God's provision then later Jethro shared something important to help Moses. What advice did Jethro give?

5. Review your first two **Memory Blessing Verses** and then add this one to help you remember God as the One who rescued His people from Egypt.

Jethro said, "Blessed be God who has delivered you from the power of Egypt and Pharaoh, who has delivered his people from the oppression of Egypt. Now I know that God is greater than all gods..." (Exodus 18:10–11a MSG)

6. Try to put yourself into this verse. Who is Jethro?

Who was Jethro talking to when he said this statement?

Where were they when this acknowledgement took place?

In what ways do you experience God as "Rescuer" or "Deliverer"?

*Paraphrase Chapter 3, **Exit and Entrance:** Leaving Egypt for the Promised Land.*

7. **Here is an example:** *God's people are saved from Egypt and enter the Promised Land. Territories were divvied up to the tribes of Israel. Judges helped God's people stay on track (but Israel failed miserably), and Ruth's love story showed God's blessings extending outside of Israel.*

8. In the story of Ruth, which character do you identify with most easily? Why?

Take some time to say aloud your paraphrased versions of Chapter 1, Chapter 2, and Chapter 3. Your wording may change each time you recount the Story, and that is okay. Your goal is to know God's Story and experience the ways God blesses. Be ready to read or tell your paraphrased version from Creation to Ruth to your study group. Put blessing to action by praying for understanding for yourself and for the others who are learning with you. Know I'm praying for you, too.

I hope that your awareness of God's blessings in your life is growing. By traveling this week along side of Moses, we are reminded that we, too, have one life to live. May we choose to live it to bless. ***Thank You God for these blessings this week:***

4

Empire

KINGDOMS ESTABLISHED

PART 1: THE LIVES OF SAUL AND DAVID

> TIME FRAME: APPROXIMATELY 1000 BC

The Empire period has lots of blessings in it so for our study Chapter 4 is divided into two parts. We begin with the birth of the prophet Samuel who anointed Israel's first king, Saul, and her second king, David. Several of David's psalms, which often direct the blessings back to God in praise, are found in this chapter. Poetry adds diversity to how God's Story is told. Chapter 4 part 1 has 51 entries from April 7 to May 27. The following ten entries provide you with the core chronological framework for the beginning of the Empire period.

Jesus,
You are the King of kings and the Lord of our hearts.
Grow us to have a heart that follows after You.
Help us learn from King David
to desire quickness to return to You when we stray away from Your ways.
Amen.

🍃

Suggested Reading from *The Blessing Book:*

🖋 APRIL 8   From Blessing a Sacrifice to Anointing a King

🖋 APRIL 11   Bless the Lord at All Times *

🖋 APRIL 18   As Peacemakers We Are Blessed

🖋 APRIL 20   Blessed Is Everyone Who Fears the Lord

🖋 MAY 4   Blessed to Have My Sins Covered

🖋 MAY 5   Blessed to Be an Upright Generation

🖋 MAY 10   Parents Are Blessed to Bless

🖋 MAY 15   Blessed Is the One Who Trusts in the Lord

🖋 MAY 21   Full Families Are a Blessing

🖋 MAY 23   Pronounce Blessings in His Name Forever

*This entry contains the memory blessing verse for Empire: Kingdoms Established.

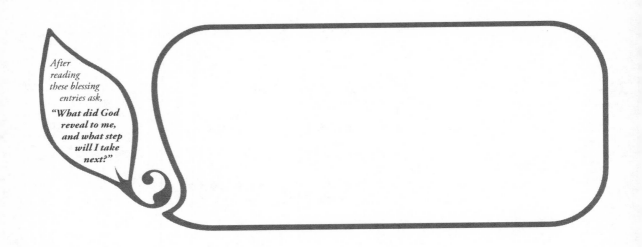

After reading these blessing entries ask,

"What did God reveal to me, and what step will I take next?"

Questions to cultivate growth:

Before he became king, David wrote Psalm 34. When loyalty to God is lived out in nations as well as in individuals, the love relationship with Holy God deepens and the ability to share blessings with others increases.

I will bless the Lord at all times; his praise shall continually be in my mouth. Oh, taste and see that the Lord is good! Blessed is the man who takes refuge in him! (Psalm 34:1, 8 ESV)

1. Read **Psalm 34** in your copy of the Bible, highlight the "bless" words, and circle the words for rescue. Reflect on what you have been rescued from and celebrate the goodness of God by thanking Him for His blessings in your life. We are rescued *from* a lot of things yet we are also rescued *to* fully love God and appropriately love people. How are you living out of your "rescued-ness"?

2. David had an interesting life from shepherd boy to king. Why do you think he is called "a man after God's heart"?

3. Practice by saying or writing out your paraphrased versions of Chapters 1–3. After Part 2 of Chapter 4, you'll paraphrase Chapter 4 and add it to your retelling of the whole biblical Story up through the Empire period.

4. Review the **Memory Blessing Verses** that you are seeking to memorize from the journey so far. Can you begin to link them together, like a story? Try it, and if you know the verses well enough to paraphrase them, your understanding will increase and the meaning will deepen. **Here are the events to help you remember the memory verses:**

   Eden (the blessing from God to be fruitful...)

   Election (Abraham was blessed to be a blessing)

   Exit and Entrance (Jethro blesses God for the rescue)

   Empire (David blesses God, then we are blessed to know God's goodness)

5. Put to practice our goal of **URU**:

**Understand
Remember
Use**

Understand: Become familiar with the overall Story of the Bible.

Remember: Link these individual accounts together through the theme of blessing as you tell the Story.

Use: Reflect on the **Eight Memory Blessing Verses** to help you see, experience, and share God's blessings.

Now be brave and tell someone else what you are learning as you journey through God's Blessings. This will increase your confidence in the process of really taking in God's Story, seeing the blessings in history and in your own life so that blessing others becomes more natural, too. Turn back to your journal pages in the Study Guide and read over some of the ways God has recently blessed you, and ways you have been a blessing to others. I believe God wants us to learn, not to just know things, *but to live more abundantly.* Let's take in His blessings and live them out.

Many of David's psalms are blessings he pours out in song to God. We have received and given blessings this week. Still keep it real, but try to record this week's blessings a little more poetically. *God, thank You for:*

4

Empire

KINGDOMS ESTABLISHED

PART 2: SOLOMON AND THE KINGDOM DIVIDED

◆ TIME FRAME: APPROXIMATELY 950 BC ◆

In this second part of Chapter 4, we are introduced to Solomon who is known for his wisdom, wealth, and power. He wrote a lot about the importance of wisdom. Sadly, at the end of his life, he chose his way over God's ways. We will also meet a few of the early prophets, and they seek to point us back to God and remind us that blessings are meant to be shared. Chapter 4 part 2 has 51 entries from May 28 to July 17. The following ten entries provide you with the core chronological framework for the life of Solomon including the Prophets who shared truth after the kingdom divided.

God,
as we live in a world that's upside-down, it can be so easy to get off track.
It is not enough to start off with honoring You,
but the real prize is to live for You our whole life through.
Help us today to learn from what the ancient prophets wrote,
so we can live with joy and purpose.
Amen.

🖋

Suggested Reading from *The Blessing Book:*

- 🖋 JUNE 6   All Praise to Jesus Whom God Has Blessed Forever
- 🖋 JUNE 7   Blessed to Find Wisdom
- 🖋 JUNE 11   Blessed to Share with Neighbors and the Poor
- 🖋 JUNE 16   Blessed to Do What Is Right
- 🖋 JUNE 27   The Valley of Blessing
- 🖋 JUNE 29   Will God Give Us a Blessing or a Curse?
- 🖋 JULY 1   Please God, Bless Our Children
- 🖋 JULY 4   Restored for Blessings
- 🖋 JULY 6   God Desires to Bless and to Lead
- 🖋 JULY 11   Blessed to Wait for God's Help

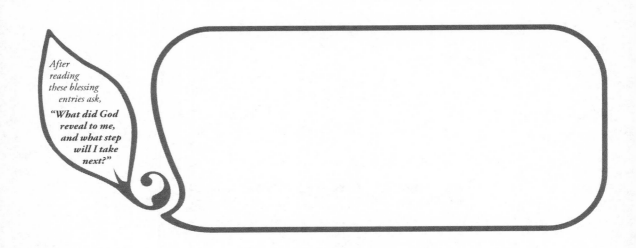

After reading these blessing entries ask, *"What did God reveal to me, and what step will I take next?"*

Questions to cultivate growth:

1. List some things about Solomon that you think might have pleased God. What are some things about Solomon that you think might not have pleased God?

2. What do you think distracted Solomon from living his whole life honoring God?

3. What do you do when distractions come in your life?

4. The prophets of God came from a variety of backgrounds, and they used different illustrations to alert their listeners. Yet most of God's prophets had the same message: "Rethink your present loyalty!" List a little something about each of the prophets we read about in the second half of Chapter 4 that help point towards living loyally.

   JOEL:

   HOSEA:

   AMOS:

   MICAH:

   ISAIAH:

5. Try to remember the **Memory Blessing Verses** which we have covered to this point in God's Story. Here are the references and some helping words to get you started:

(Eden) Genesis 1:28 NLT

Then God _____ them and said, "Be _____ and _____. Fill the earth and _____ it. _____ over the _____ _____ _____ _____, the birds in the sky, and all the _____ that scurry along the ground."

(Election) Genesis 12:2–3 NIV

"I will make you into a great _____, and I will _____ you; I will make your _____ great, and you will be a _____. I will _____ those who _____ you, and whoever curses you I will curse; and all _____ on earthwill be _____ through you."

(Exit and Entrance) Exodus 18:10–11a MSG

Jethro said, " _____ be God who has _____ you from the power of _____ and Pharaoh, who has delivered his people from the _____ of Egypt. Now I know that God is _____ than all _____ …"

(Empire) Psalms 34:1, 8 ESV

I will _____ the _____ at all _____; his _____ shall continually be in my _____.

Oh, taste and _____ that the _____ is good! _____ is the man who takes refuge in _____!

6. For a fresh review of where we are heading in the journey, read the rest of the **Memory Blessing Verses** to complete God's blessing Story.

5 **Exile:** Into Captivity and Back Again
JEREMIAH 31:2, 23 NLT

This is what the Lord says: "Those who survive the coming destruction will find blessings even in the barren land, for I will give rest to the people of Israel."

This is what the Lord of Heaven's Armies, the God of Israel, says: "When I bring them back from captivity, the people of Judah and its towns will again say, 'The Lord bless you, O righteous home, O holy mountain!'"

6 **Emmanuel:** God with Us through Jesus
MATTHEW 5:3–10 NIV

Blessed are the poor in spirit, for theirs is the kingdom of heaven.

Blessed are those who mourn, for they will be comforted.

Blessed are the meek, for they will inherit the earth.

Blessed are those who hunger and thirst for righteousness, for they will be filled.

Blessed are the merciful, for they will be shown mercy.

Blessed are the pure in heart, for they will see God.

Blessed are the peacemakers, for they will be called children of God.

Blessed are those who are persecuted because of righteousness, for theirs is the kingdom of heaven.

7 **Exhortation:** Letters to Encourage and Inspire
ROMANS 10:12–13 NIV

For there is no difference between Jew and Gentile—the same Lord is Lord of all and richly blesses all who call on him, for, "Everyone who calls on the name of the Lord will be saved."

8 **Eternity:** The Best Is yet to Come
REVELATION 7:12 NLT

"Amen! Blessing and glory and wisdom and thanksgiving and honor and power and strength belong to our God forever and ever! Amen."

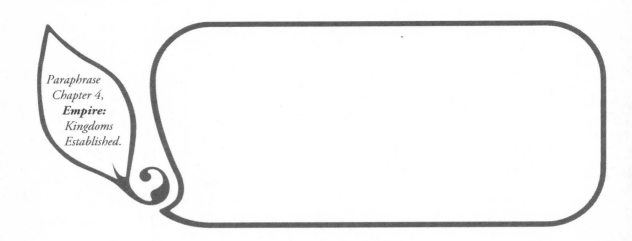

*Paraphrase Chapter 4, **Empire:** Kingdoms Established.*

7. The first four events from Eden through Empire give us a lot of history to think through. List these events. We will learn from one more major event (Exit and Return) before we arrive at the New Testament.

1) ___ **EDEN** ___

2) _____

3) _____

4) _____

Congratulations! We have made it to the mid-way point in our journey together. I trust that God is growing you more and more into His character as you stand in the stream of living water, receiving His blessings and blessing others in your days. Be sure to pray for those in your blessing study group; let's not grow weary or lose heart! Press on in God's goodness because the next road we will travel down is very challenging for God's people. It reminds us of the truth that when we take a detour from God's way, our destination may not be what we had hoped.

It is hard to be a blessing or receive gifts from God if we are off track with Him, or others. Take a minute or so to reflect, and if need be, make things right. *With renewed loyalty, thank God for the goodness restoration brings:*

5

Exile and Return

INTO CAPTIVITY AND BACK AGAIN

TIME FRAME: APPROXIMATELY 500 BC

God blessed His people so that they would be a blessing to other nations, but sadly they did not bless people of other nations (or the poor within their own communities). It took a lot to get their attention: enemy captivity, wisdom spoken through the prophets, hardships, and God's relentless love for His people. For some, their hearts of stone were changed to hearts of flesh and restoration to God happened. Chapter 5 has 37 entries from July 18 to August 22. The following ten entries provide you with the core chronological framework for the events of the Exile and the captives return to Jerusalem. As we read this portion of history, let's be sure to open up to God where we are in our present day. Maybe we are not physically in Babylon, but are we in some kind of exile, held captive by sin?

Lord,
please shine Your light in our hearts. Are we living in ways
that Your love moves through us or have we, like the Israelites before us,
yielded to selfishness which blocks the flow of blessings?
Lord, please free us to fully love.
Amen.

Suggested Reading from *The Blessing Book:*

🍃	JULY 18	Actively Seek God's Blessings
🍃	JULY 25	Bless the God of Heaven
🍃	JULY 27	Blessings Will Come Back *
🍃	JULY 30	Blessed to Give Firstly to God
🍃	AUGUST 3	Blessed to Be Corrected
🍃	AUGUST 8	An Appalling Blessing
🍃	AUGUST 11	Make God Our Priority; Blessings Will Come
🍃	AUGUST 12	May God Bless the Temple Again
🍃	AUGUST 16	Heed the Lord's Warning; Cursed Blessings Are Not Good
🍃	AUGUST 22	Bless the Lord from Everlasting to Everlasting

*This entry contains the memory blessing verse for Exile and Return: Into Captivity and Back Again.

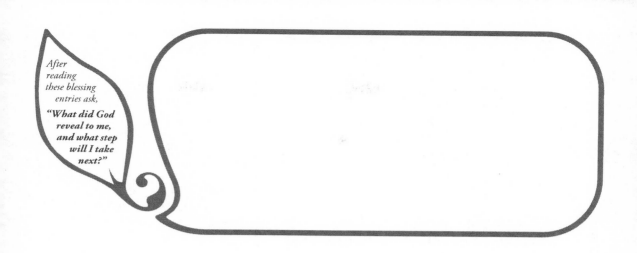

After reading these blessing entries ask,

"What did God reveal to me, and what step will I take next?"

Questions to cultivate growth:

1. Many kings ruled during this period of history. At this point the kingdom is divided, and all nations continued to struggle. Several prophets sought to turn the hearts of God's people back to Him. List something that helps you to learn the importance of loyalty to God as you read how these men of God lived and what they proclaimed.

   ZEPHANIAH:

   DANIEL:

   JEREMIAH:

   EZEKIEL:

   HAGGAI:

   ZECHARIAH:

   MALACHI:

2. Most people are familiar with Job who is associated with faithful suffering. God's people were suffering in captivity and Job's story brought encouragement. Describe a characteristic of Job that you value, or something fresh God has shown you from the life of Job.

3. Some suffering can be avoided because some of it is linked to the consequences of disobedience like the suffering many of the Israelites were facing. Job was righteous, yet he suffered. His suffering came as a test. Would he curse God and die or would he press on bravely, honoring God with his words and actions? As you journey through life how do you respond when suffering comes?

4. Jesus suffered, and so did many of those who have faithfully followed Him throughout history. What are your views on suffering? Who do you know personally who has suffered in ways that honor God in their specific situation?

5. Jeremiah, a prophet who foretold the new covenant, also explained destruction and restoration for the Israelites. *Jeremiah 31* gives great hope. Prayerfully read it in your Bible and be sure to highlight the blessing words in verses 2 and 23.

This is what the Lord says: "Those who survive the coming destruction will find blessings even in the barren land, for I will give rest to the people of Israel."

This is what the Lord of Heaven's Armies, the God of Israel, says: "When I bring them back from captivity, the people of Judah and its towns will again say, 'The Lord bless you, O righteous home, O holy mountain!'" (Jeremiah 31:2, 23 NLT)

6. It is sad that many of the consequences that God made clear back in the time of Moses, if His people chose to break their covenant with Him, are now coming about. Use the space below to summarize this tragic, yet hopeful period of history.

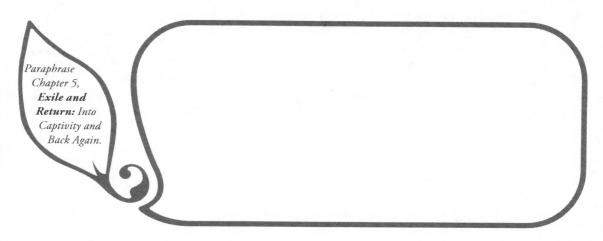

Paraphrase Chapter 5, **Exile and Return:** *Into Captivity and Back Again.*

7. Think about the events leading up to the Exile and the eventual return from it. Fill in the blanks with the main character or the event, gaining awareness of the trek we have been on through God's Story from the beginning to the end of the Old Testament.

EDEN: Adam and Eve

ELECTION: _____

_____ : **Moses and then Joshua**

_____ : **Saul,** _____ , **and Solomon**

_____ : **many Prophets**

Here is what awaits us in the New Testament:

EMMANUEL: Jesus

EXHORTATION: Paul and other letter writers

ETERNITY: The Blessed One revealed

Keep practicing your Memory Blessing Verses as your understanding of the sequence of God's Story deepens. These verses will help keep you grounded in His Word and in His blessings. Look to the tips on page 60 for continued help as you seek to take His Word to heart. As we journey onward in God's Story, let's pause and take a look at where we have already been. The road before us has mountains yet to climb. We can gain momentum as we look back on where God has taken us through in the past. He is our faithful Guide.

8.   Have fun with a little review of our journey.

Who receives God's blessing in *Genesis 1:28*? _____

In *Genesis 12:2–3* God blesses _____ to be a blessing.

Jethro is talking to Moses in *Exodus 18:10–11a* and says, "...blessed be _____ for the wonderful deliverance He has provided. He is the best!"

I love how *Psalm 34:1* and *8* bless both God and humanity! I will bless the _____ at all times... Blessed is the _____ who takes refuge in Him!

It is God who is again blessing His people in *Jeremiah 31:2* while they are in captivity and in *Jeremiah 31:23* when He brings them back from it. Although disobedience has consequences, God faithfully restores His people.

This period ends with a 400 plus-year silence before we meet the Leading Character in God's Story. I think Chapter 6 is my favorite chapter because I love Jesus and I love learning from Him. Get ready to encounter the goodness, grace, and truth of Emmanuel, God with us. Jesus is our ultimate traveling companion and He promises to be with us until the end of time and beyond. Be sure to tighten the straps of your sandals; we are about to climb to hear afresh Jesus' sermon on the mount!

Seeking to understand the blessings experienced by God's people through history makes us more aware of how we, as God's people in this day, are called to be a blessing. *Thank You God for using me to bless this week:*

6

Emmanuel

GOD WITH US THROUGH JESUS

◆ ▰ **TIME FRAME: APPROXIMATELY 5 BC** ▰ ◆

There is no doubt about it, Jesus is the Main Character in God's Story. We are all blessed by His life and His resurrection from the dead that gives us New Life. His teaching offers us wisdom, His interactions with people model strength and compassion, and He shows us the importance of time spent with His Father in prayer. Chapter 6 has 50 entries from August 23 to October 11. For our study, we will focus primarily on Jesus' teaching from His sermon on the mount. I hope you will take the time to read through all of Chapter 6 as the more we know about Jesus, the more we can grow to be like Him. As you read, look for the many ways Jesus lived out the Beatitudes in His life.

Jesus,
please bless us as we seek to know You.
May it be Your light that shines through us
as we live out the gift of life that You give.
Guide us, open us up to seeing more of You, please come near to us we pray.
Amen.

🍃

Suggested Reading from *The Blessing Book:*

- 🖎 AUGUST 23   Mary Received a Shocking Blessing
- 🖎 SEPTEMBER 1   Blessings on the Poor in Spirit *
- 🖎 SEPTEMBER 2   Blessed to Be Comforted after Mourning *
- 🖎 SEPTEMBER 3   The Humble are Blessed *
- 🖎 SEPTEMBER 4   Pursuing Righteousness is a Blessing *
- 🖎 SEPTEMBER 5   Mercy—Blessed to Receive, Blessed to Give *
- 🖎 SEPTEMBER 6   Blessed to See God *
- 🖎 SEPTEMBER 7   Blessed to Be a Peacemaker *
- 🖎 SEPTEMBER 8   The Persecuted Ones Are Blessed *
- 🖎 OCTOBER 10   Blessed Are Those Who Have Not Seen yet Believe

These entries contains the memory blessing verses for Emmanuel: God with Us through Jesus.

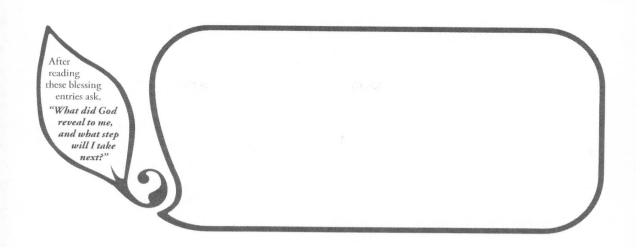

After reading these blessing entries ask, *"What did God reveal to me, and what step will I take next?"*

Questions to cultivate growth:

1. Prayerfully read through **Matthew 5** in your Bible and highlight "blessed" in Jesus' sermon on the mount. Jesus models what it means to be blessed and it does not always look like what we might think.

   Our **Memory Blessing Verses** for Chapter 6, Emmanuel: God with Us through Jesus are:

   Blessed are the poor in spirit, for theirs is the kingdom of heaven.

   Blessed are those who mourn, for they will be comforted.

   Blessed are the meek, for they will inherit the earth.

   Blessed are those who hunger and thirst for righteousness, for they will be filled.

   Blessed are the merciful, for they will be shown mercy.

   Blessed are the pure in heart, for they will see God.

   Blessed are the peacemakers, for they will be called children of God.

   Blessed are those who are persecuted because of righteousness, for theirs is the kingdom of heaven.

   (Matthew 5:3–10 NIV)

Jesus' followers remain amazed by His teaching. As you put this longer passage to memory, pray for God to help you really let it all sink into your being, so your actions can change to be more like His. Look to Jesus because He is an example to us for each of the situations that lead to being blessed.

2. **Here are the first four blessings:**

Blessed are the _____ in spirit, for theirs is the _____

of _____ .

Blessed are those who _____ , for they will be comforted.

Blessed are the meek, for they will _____ the _____ .

Blessed are those who _____ and _____ for

righteousness, for they will be _____ .

3. **Get the first four beatitudes down and then add the next four to them:**

Blessed are the _____ , for they will be shown mercy.

Blessed are the _____ in heart, for they will see _____ .

Blessed are the peacemakers, for the will be called _____

of _____ .

Blessed are those who are _____ because of righteousness, for

theirs is the _____ of _____ .

4. Jesus teaches us that we are blessed to receive, and we are blessed when we give. At the end of the Gospel according to Luke, Jesus tells the importance of knowing God's full Story. Paraphrase Chapter 6, God with Us through Jesus, in one to three sentences. Then start at the beginning with Eden and link all the events together up through Emmanuel. Share your paraphrased highlights with someone this week.

Paraphrase Chapter 6, **Emmanuel:** *God With Us Through Jesus.*

We are making progress on knowing the verses that help us know the Story. Try saying the memory verses in the morning before you get out of bed, or as you walk along in your day, or maybe as you eat your meals, or as you lay back down at the end of the day. Making scripture memorization a discipline that we value helps us to stay aware of our God who blesses us. Adding the Memory Blessing Verses to your paraphrased retelling of each of the Eight Events will strengthen your understanding of God's Story. Remember: you are a part of this Good Story!

5. Write the scripture reference for each of the six major events of God's Story that we have studied so far.

   EDEN: *Genesis 1:28*

   ELECTION:

   EXIT AND ENTRANCE:

   EMPIRE:

   EXILE AND RETURN:

   EMMANUEL:

   We have two more major events to learn from:

   EXILE AND RETURN: *Romans 10:12–13*

   EMMANUEL: *Revelation 7:12*

Good job on growing in your awareness of God's Story! Knowing the "address" of each verse can help us to find it quickly when we want to learn more details for ourselves or to locate the verses when sharing with others. With Jesus beside us and leading us forward, we continue on in our trek through God's blessings. How about a little rest, hopefully under a shade tree; with cold, clean water to refresh us. Jesus is Living Water. Enjoy a break with a crossword puzzle that grows our awareness of His goodness.

JESUS: A Friend Worth Knowing

ACROSS

2 Involved with Jesus' first miracle
5 Blessed to inherit the earth
8 Directed Joseph several times
9 Said, "It is more blessed to give than to receive"
14 Opened by Jesus in Emmaus
15 Brought the first blessing of the N.T.
17 A gift Jesus offers His friends
19 Number of loaves blessed at feeding of 5000
21 Found for our souls when we take Jesus' yoke
22 The woman with bleeding had this
23 He led them as far as _____ and blessed them
24 Said, "You are blessed because you believed...."
26 Blessed to be called children of God
27 Jesus is the best _____
28 Jesus took these in His arms and blessed
29 Recorded Jesus' sermon on the mount

DOWN

1 We are to appropriately _____ God and people
3 Proclaimed, "My Lord and my God!"
4 Love the Lord with heart, soul, strength, _____
6 What to do when others curse you
7 Jesus is the _____ - King
10 Took Jesus in his arms and blessed Him
11 Said, "You are the Messiah...."
12 Will be shown mercy
13 An expression of adoration we give to Jesus
16 Jesus was born here
18 Blessed above all women
20 Where Jesus celebrated Passover
25 Jesus' cousin

 Let's never get too old to be like 28 across.

Jesus is love and we were created to be loving. Let's love like Jesus in both big and little ways. *Jesus, You are the best blessing I know! Thank You for these specific blessings I have experienced this week. I'm also grateful for the ways I have been a blessing to others:*

7

Exhortation

LETTERS TO ENCOURAGE AND INSPIRE

PART 1: THE EARLY CHURCH AND PAUL

TIME FRAME: APPROXIMATELY AD 35

God's blessings flow through men like Peter and Paul and the young church forms and grows. Acts records the action of the Holy Spirit moving through people who share the Good News. We will focus on Paul in the first half of Chapter 7. He is the most influential emissary of the early church and is a prolific letter writer who offers relevant guidance in Christian growth. Chapter 7 part 1 has 55 entries from October 12 to December 5. The following ten entries provide you with the core chronological framework of Paul's letters.

Lord Jesus,
it is You we want to be like.
May our love, wisdom and desire to choose what is right expand as we move on in maturity. When we encounter things in our character that do not line up with Yours,
please give us the desire and courage and strength to change.
Amen.

Suggested Reading from *The Blessing Book:*

- OCTOBER 18   Those Who Have Faith Are Blessed
- OCTOBER 24   Glorious Blessedness yet to Come
- OCTOBER 31   Cup of Blessing
- NOVEMBER 13   God Blesses All Who Call on Him *
- NOVEMBER 22   Blessing and Peace from God
- NOVEMBER 25   God's Best; Christ's Blessings
- NOVEMBER 26   Adopted and Blessed
- NOVEMBER 29   Rejoice Again with Blessings
- DECEMBER 2   God Is Our Blessed and Only Sovereign
- DECEMBER 3   Blessed Hope; Jesus Returning

*This entry contains the memory blessing verse for Exhortation: Letters to Encourage and Inspire.

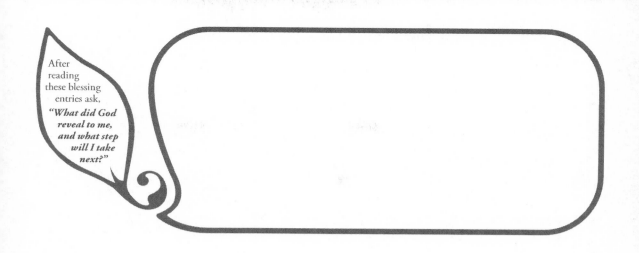

Questions to cultivate growth:

1. In Chapter 7 we will cover a lot of ground for Paul was a traveling man. He wrote to many churches and individuals who became dear to him along the way, and we read bits of those letters, seeing the blessings he shared. Emphasize something that can bring about maturity.

    Here is an example:

    GALATIANS: *remember people are blessed through faith.*

    THESSALONIANS:

    CORINTHIANS:

    ROMANS:

    COLOSSIANS:

    PHILEMON:

    EPHESIANS:

    PHILIPPIANS:

    TIMOTHY:

    TITUS:

2. If you were alive during Paul's time, which church would you like to have been a member of? Why?

3. When Paul writes to the church in Rome, he quotes quite a few of the Old Testament prophets. Paul knew God's Story. Joel is quoted in our memory verse to help us with what Paul sought to teach:

   For there is no difference between Jew and Gentile—the same Lord is Lord of all and richly blesses all who call on him, for, "Everyone who calls on the name of the Lord will be saved." (Romans 10:12–13 NIV)

   If you have called on Jesus, how are you richly blessed?

4. In your own Bible, read **Romans 10** and highlight "blesses" when you come to the twelfth verse. Think back on the blessing promise given to Abraham. In what ways was that blessing promise being extended in Paul's lifetime?

5. Review your version of God's Story from Creation up through Paul. Practice adding in your **Memory Blessing Verses** for each of the events. Knowing scripture well enough to paraphrase it can really help us get closer to our goal that scripture would become useful in our everyday lives. Share the Blessing Story to someone new this week.

> **Give thanks to God for specific ways He has blessed you recently. The NIV version of our latest Memory Blessing Verse uses the words "richly blesses" while The Voice says, "…He is Lord over all things, and He pours out His treasures…" A rich pouring out of treasures on those who call out to the Lord is a wonderful blessing! May you be encouraged to live in God's blessings and extend blessings to others. "…let's not get tired of doing what is good. At just the right time we will reap a harvest of blessing if we don't give up" Galatians 6:9 NLT.**

God, thank You for continually growing me through the letters Your leaders have written. Here are some of my blessings this week, those I received and those that I gave:

7

Exhortation

LETTERS TO ENCOURAGE AND INSPIRE

PART 2: ADDITIONAL NEW TESTAMENT GUIDANCE

▶ TIME FRAME: APPROXIMATELY AD 35 ◀

In the second half of Chapter 7 we read letters from a variety of leaders to bless the growing movement of churches that follow Jesus. Each of these leaders sought to communicate the importance of healthy relationships both with God and with people. Years later, we are blessed to learn from those who walked with Jesus and heard His teachings first-hand. Chapter 7 part 2 has 16 entries from December 6 to December 21. The following ten entries provide you with the core chronological framework for the additional helpful letters that make up the New Testament.

Father God,
help us to never grow tired of learning Your ways
as Your ways are the way we need for a life of hope, love, and purpose.
Please grow us up. Grow our strength, our faith, and our love in action.
Amen.

🌿

Suggested Reading from *The Blessing Book:*

🌿	DECEMBER 6	Blessed with the Crown of Life
🌿	DECEMBER 8	Do Blessings Flow from Us?
🌿	DECEMBER 10	Don't Pervert God's Blessings into Lawlessness
🌿	DECEMBER 11	Blessed to Be Born Again
🌿	DECEMBER 12	Payback Blessings
🌿	DECEMBER 14	Blessed When Insulted Because of Jesus
🌿	DECEMBER 15	Blessings like Rain
🌿	DECEMBER 17	Blessing Giver is Greater Than Blessing Receiver
🌿	DECEMBER 18	Bless Those Who Come after Us
🌿	DECEMBER 20	Blessed to Have Eternal Life

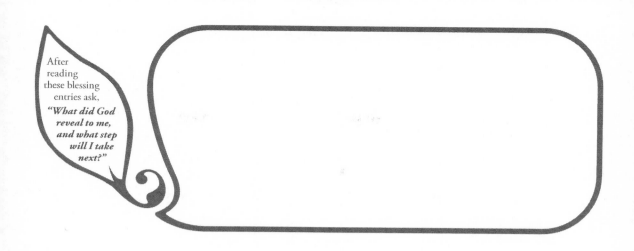

After reading these blessing entries ask, *"What did God reveal to me, and what step will I take next?"*

Questions to cultivate growth:

1. List the 5 authors mentioned in the second part of Chapter 7. Include who they were writing to, and jot down a few blessings that these leaders shared.

Here is an example:

James wrote to Jewish believers.

BLESSINGS:
- Blessed with the crown of life when we do not cave in to trials.
- Blessed to actually live out the law of freedom.
- Blessed if we use our mouth to bless, not curse.

Jude wrote to _____.

BLESSINGS:

P_____ wrote to _____.

BLESSINGS:

Unknown Author wrote to the Hebrews (Jewish believers).

BLESSINGS:

J_____ wrote to _____.

BLESSINGS:

2. How can you apply these blessings to this season in your life? Look over the **Action Options** on pages 68–77 for help with making meaningful applications. Indicate a few of the Action Options that you would like to make progress with that relate to your desired character growth. Where have you seen growth so far, and what habit or change do you feel God would like for you to make next?

3. You know what to do!

Paraphrase Chapter 7, **Exhortation: Letters to Encourage and Inspire** *(1 & 2).*

4. We have only one more chapter in our study, make sure you stay hydrated on our journey! Take some time this week to drink in the **Memory Blessing Verses** you have learned so far. To get your mind flowing, match the Events with the References and then number the Events from 1 (Eden) to 8 (Eternity).

ETERNITY   *Psalms 34:1, 8*

EXIT AND ENTRANCE   *Genesis 12:2–3*

EMPIRE   *Genesis 1:28*

EMMANUEL   *Exodus 18:10*

EXILE AND RETURN   *Revelation 7:12*

EDEN   *Matthew 5:3–10*

EXHORTATION   *Jeremiah 31:2, 23*

ELECTION   *Romans 10:12–13*

Tell yourself the good story of God's good blessings. Start in the beginning when God blessed Adam and Eve, onto the blessing of Abraham, through to the the great escape from Egypt, and the entrance into the Promised Land. God's blessings continued as the kingdom was established, and we saw the consequence of exile because God's blessings where not shared. Thankful for the blessing of restoration, we met the Main Character in His Story, and we read letters written to bless the followers of Jesus. Eternity awaits us. God has placed eternity in the human heart, yet we can not understand everything that He has done and will do. His Story shows us His good character and His desire to bless. We experience His blessings in our lives, and we bless Him when we choose to bless others while living gratefully. Each day is a choice: do we adventure forward intentionally living out God's plan of blessing in our lives or choose a lesser path?

We do not control all the circumstance along the way, but we are given grace to live purposefully in our days. *Father, I thank You for this week's blessings which help me know You better. Here are a few ways I have shared Your blessings with others:*

8

Eternity

THE BEST IS YET TO COME

TIME FRAME: WRITTEN APPROXIMATELY AD 95

The destination in our journey through blessings takes us right back to God who is the giver of every good blessing throughout time. This final chapter is an exciting conclusion to a fascinating Story. God's faithfulness is trustworthy, throughout history, and throughout our days. What awaits us is beyond our imagination even better than all the blessings this world holds. Our journey comes to an end, yet the end is where the real beginning starts.

Our Father,
thank You for Your many blessings:
Your goodness experienced through
forgiveness, adoption and identity, and purpose in our lives.
You have created us, redeemed us and lovingly sustain us.
Thank You Father for Jesus, the Author and Completer of our faith
and for Your Holy Spirt as a Faithful Guide that lives within us.
Amen.

Suggested Reading from *The Blessing Book:*

- DECEMBER 22   Blessed When We Read Revelation
- DECEMBER 23   Blessed Be the Lamb Forever!
- DECEMBER 24   Blessing and so Much More Belong to God *
- DECEMBER 25   God Blesses All Who Call on Him
- DECEMBER 26   Blessed Are the Watchful Ones
- DECEMBER 27   God's Best; Christ's Blessings
- DECEMBER 28   Blessed Resurrection
- DECEMBER 29   Amazing Blessings to Inherit
- DECEMBER 30   God Is Our Blessed and Only Sovereign
- DECEMBER 31   Blessed to Receive the Tree of Life

*This entry contains the memory blessing verse for Eternity: The Best Is yet to Come.

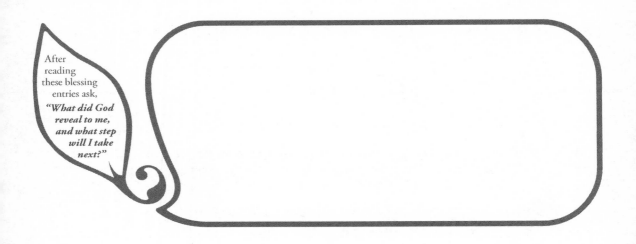

Qustions to cultivate growth:

1. Who wrote The Revelation of Jesus Christ?

2. What are some of the blessings that await those who trust in Jesus that you are particularly excited about?

3. Read **Revelation 7** in your Bible and highlight "blessing" in verse twelve. Revelation 7:12 gives us a glimpse of our final destination. All blessing belongs to God who is worthy of all our praise!

    "Amen! Blessing and glory and wisdom and thanksgiving and honor and power and strength belong to our God forever and ever! Amen." (Revelation 7:12 NLT)

    From our final memory verse, list the things that belong to God.

    BLESSING belongs to God

    G _____

    W _____

    T _____

    H _____

    P _____

    S _____

4. Add the phrase, "belongs to God" next to the words you have written about God. Out of the seven attributes that describe aspects of God and His character, which are you most easily able to relate to?

5. Write out the scripture references for each of the Eight Events that make up God's Story of blessings. As you do this, record or say out loud, the verses that match each of the references, picturing what took place in these distinct events. Even though our study is coming to a close, you will continue to be blessed as you build on the framework of knowing God's Story.

Example:

EDEN: *(Genesis 2:18) Then God blessed them and said, "Be fruitful and multiply. Fill the earth and govern it. Reign over the fish in the sea, the birds in the sky and all the animals that scurry along the ground." (Genesis 2:18)*

ELECTION:

EXIT AND ENTRANCE:

EMPIRE:

EXILE AND RETURN:

EMMANUEL:

EXHORTATION:

ETERNITY:

6. Write your final paraphrase below.

*Paraphrase Chapter 8, **Eternity:** The Best Is Yet to Come.*

Now that you have added your paraphrased finale to God's Story of blessings, be sure to share your version of Eden through to Eternity with someone this week. Even if what you do is say, "Hi, I'm learning God's Story in Eight Events that focus on blessings. As part of my homework I need to share it with someone. May I tell it to you?" The more we share the Story, the more we know the Story, which increases our desire to live out appropriate love.

As you go through your day, think about ways that knowing God's faithfulness is a blessing to you. Rejoice often in your adoption into God's family and choose to live in loyal royal-ness, as a child of the King. As we share God's blessings we are living out, "His will be done, His Kingdom come, here like how things are in Heaven."

Understand

Remember

Use

Put **URU** to good practice by concluding this study with strength. Consider **URU** as a format to help you with future times of growth and learning. The more we fully **understand** something the better we are able to really **remembering** it. Taking principles we **understand** and **remember** can grow our desired character. **URU**, *you are you*, God designed you uniquely and we each have a role to play in His Story. Knowing our identity and effectively **using** our giftedness increases our **usefulness** and joy of living in God's Kingdom.

God's Story is rich in blessings for He richly blesses! Our blessing quest has covered many years and many pages, yet the pursuit of God and love is never-ending. Growth in Him is lifelong and life-changing. May God richly bless you as you continue on your journey with Him, getting to know Him better and better. His stream of blessing flows to all generations—let's live with wet feet, being actively involved. Throughout history we have seen specific ways God has blessed His people; may we see our lives as opportunities from Him to be a blessing, knowing we are wonderfully blessed!

I pray for you my friend,
that God our Father and Lord Jesus Christ
will be so kind to you
and will pour out treasures of BLESSINGS on you,
especially giving you peace!
Ephesians 1:2

(paraphrased by kkm)

Look back over some of your recorded blessings during the course of this journey through God's Story. *Conclude by recording a few of the blessings you have given and received this week, thanking God for them.*

Go forth in blessings; to bless God and people.

Eight Memory Blessing Verses

The Bible is a big book! One of our goals in this study is to know the flow of the whole biblical Story. The following eight passages describe particular aspects of the events that take place chronologically in God's Story. With Jesus as our foundation, the **Eight Memory Blessing Verses** are used as a structure to more meaningfully understand what the Bible is all about. When we see our lives lived within the framework of God's Story, we gain wisdom which is useful to us and for others, and can bring joy to God. A healthy outcome of knowing God's Story can be to more consistently live in joyful obedience. The blessings of God begin at the very beginning and extend to eternity. Let's know them and live them out in our lifetime as we love God and love people.

1 Eden: Where It All Begins
GENESIS 1:28 NLT

Then God blessed them and said, "Be fruitful and multiply. Fill the earth and govern it. Reign over the fish in the sea, the birds in the sky, and all the animals that scurry along the ground."

2 Election: Abraham's Blessing Extends to Blessing the World
GENESIS 12:2–3 NIV

"I will make you into a great nation, and I will bless you; I will make your name great, and you will be a blessing. I will bless those who bless you, and whoever curses you I will curse; and all peoples on earth will be blessed through you."

3 Exit and Entrance: Leaving Egypt for the Promised Land
EXODUS 18:10–11A MSG

Jethro said, "Blessed be God who has delivered you from the power of Egypt and Pharaoh, who has delivered his people from the oppression of Egypt. Now I know that God is greater than all gods…"

4 Empire: Kingdoms Established
PSALM 34:1, 8 ESV

I will bless the Lord at all times; his praise shall continually be in my mouth.

Oh, taste and see that the Lord is good! Blessed is the man who takes refuge in him!

5 Exile and Return: Into Captivity and Back Again
JEREMIAH 31:2, 23 NLT

This is what the Lord says: "Those who survive the coming destruction will find blessings even in the barren land, for I will give rest to the people of Israel."

This is what the Lord of Heaven's Armies, the God of Israel, says: "When I bring them back from captivity, the people of Judah and its towns will again say, 'The Lord bless you, O righteous home, O holy mountain!'"

6 Emmanuel: God with Us through Jesus
MATTHEW 5:3–10 NIV

Blessed are the poor in spirit, for theirs is the kingdom of heaven.

Blessed are those who mourn, for they will be comforted.

Blessed are the meek, for they will inherit the earth.

Blessed are those who hunger and thirst for righteousness, for they will be filled.

Blessed are the merciful, for they will be shown mercy.

Blessed are the pure in heart, for they will see God.

Blessed are the peacemakers, for they will be called children of God.

Blessed are those who are persecuted because of righteousness, for theirs is the kingdom of heaven.

7 Exhortation: Letters to Encourage and Inspire
ROMANS 10:12–13 NIV

For there is no difference between Jew and Gentile—the same Lord is Lord of all and richly blesses all who call on him, for, "Everyone who calls on the name of the Lord will be saved."

8 Eternity: The Best Is yet to Come
REVELATION 7:12 NLT

"Amen! Blessing and glory and wisdom and thanksgiving and honor and power and strength belong to our God forever and ever! Amen."

Make It Yours: Scripture Memorization
Tips for the Eight Memory Blessing Verses

Memorization used to be a skill we needed to use to remember addresses, phone numbers, special dates and even math facts. Electronic devices have helped us keep up with a very complex world, yet in some ways those devices have undermined our needed ability to actively engage in memorization. For this study we will seek to memorize eight passages (some longer than others) which provide us with the outline for the whole biblical Story. This is not an easy undertaking. We need to count the cost and know why we desire to make such an investment. What will be gained by taking to heart the knowledge of God and what He says about His Story? The following tips can help us to really internalize what it is we want to remember when it comes to God's Story so that the application to our own life stories can be more meaningful. We are individuals with different leaning styles so hopefully you can find what will aid you in your goal to make it your own.

℮ **WRITE** the verse on a note card to carry with you or put it in a place where you see it often so you can reflect on it throughout the day. I find it helpful to keep all eight of the **Memory Blessing Verses** on a small hoop. For some people, writing the verse over and over will help it to sink in, or you might find that typing it out at various times during the day may increase your ability to remember it. Other people find it helpful to act out the verses which can cement the verses into the mind. **Example: *The Eden Event is the prelude to God's Story of blessings. Genesis 1:28 talks of reigning over fish in the sea (hand motion like ocean waves), birds in the sky (hand motion like flying) then concludes with "...all the animals that scurry along the ground." When I walk or ride my bike and see squirrels, rabbits, cats, and at times animals I wish I had not seen, I think about how God blessed mankind to care for and properly govern (have dominion) over even scurrying animals.***

℮ **REPEAT** your **Memory Blessing Verses** at night before going to sleep, or as a part of your meals, or while driving, exercising, cleaning house, any time!

Having set times, or linking the verses to an activity, helps maintain a daily discipline toward the goal of putting the verse to memory and then from memory to living out godly principles. The blessing principle established as far back as the life of Abraham during the Election Event can give great structure to what is important in our day-to-day now. **Example:** *Genesis 12:2–3 uses "bless" five times. As you go through your day, reflect how you have been blessed by God, for things like the bed you sleep in, the food you eat, health to do what you do, and then seek to bless others, remembering the conclusion of the promise: "all peoples on earth will be blessed through you."*

℃ **THINK** about the **who, what, when, where, why** and **how** of a particular verse because those details may actually help you in the process of making the verse your own. We often engage best with a verse when we get curious about it so try to put yourself in the situation of the verse. **Example:** *Exodus 18:10–11a is one man's exclamation after hearing an amazing rescue story of God's power and care at the time of the Exit and Entrance Event. Who is doing the talking and who is doing the listening? What happened and what can I learn about God from this situation? When and where did this take place in time and space? Why is this exclamation important? Does this give me a clue to themes within God's bigger Story? How does knowing this particular truth help me as I live out my story?*

℃ **PONDER** the writing style of the verses you want to memorize. Is the verse a command, poetry, a prayer? Is it descriptive or prescriptive? Is it about an event yet to come? Tone of voice makes a big difference in our conversations and when we look we can discover the tone of voice in these ancient written words too. **Example:** *Psalm 34 was created as a prayer or praise song by David during the Empire Event. David was not yet the ruling king when he penned this chorus to God. He expressed how God is worthy to be blessed, and we are blessed when we know He is good! In Psalm 34:1 and 8, David poetically uses "mouth" in two ways. First he says that praise is to be the sound coming from our mouth, and second, how our mouth is involved to taste and know what is good.*

℃ **READ** the whole chapter or at least the verses before and after the specific **Memory Blessing Verse**, so you can better picture what is taking place. Underline the memory verses in your Bible, highlight the words used for "bless," and remember that each of our eight passages links to the next in the chronological story. **Example:** *Reading all of Jeremiah 31 (from the Exile and Return Event) will fill in a whole lot of detail that then gives understanding to the blessings found in that challenging time in history. When we read our blessing verses (Jeremiah 31:2 and 23) in context and put them to memory, we have truth ready to reflect on when we are in need of focusing on God's goodness in our challenges. We can quickly choose to turn to Him. This gives us real hope as we live in the real world.*

☾ **PRAY** the verse you are trying to memorize for yourself and for others as it is applicable. As you commit more verses to memory, pray for more people and their needs. This really does then take the verses from your head to your heart and from your heart to God's. **Example:** *When praying through the beatitudes (Matthew 5:3–10, the teachings from the life of Emmanuel), the verses turned to prayer can be like: "God, M is mourning the death of his father, please bless him with your comfort. J is hungry and thirsty for your righteousness, help him Lord to know that in You he will have blessed satisfaction. God, I struggle with being pure in heart, may I treasure the blessing of seeing You above all else. Thank you for P who is such a peacemaker at work, please grow her in knowing she is Your child... ."*

☾ **PRACTICE** your **Memory Blessing Verses** with someone else and ask them to check your accuracy by looking at your memory cards. Prompters such as the Event or the scripture reference are good ways to prime the memory pump. It is even more effective to get a partner who also values learning the verses so you can practice them together. Shared ownership can build confidence. Talking about the principles from the verses and how they make a difference in your life can help form healthy habits. Looking for opportunities to share your verses with others in conversation, emails, etc. furthers your desire to know God's blessings and to bless others. **Example:** *In the Exhortation Event we see how Paul wrote many letters. His succinct way of expressing God's blessing for all people in Romans 10:12–13 can help motivate us to actively share with the people in our realm of influence. We all need to be saved, to be rescued, to be brought into a life of rich blessing. Take joy in being one God uses to spread the Good News!*

C SAY the verse out loud, or sing it and include the scripture reference. Hearing our own voice with our own ears is a great learning technique. Say the verse's address at the beginning of the verse and then again at the end to help remember the reference. Emphasizing different words in the verse as you say the verse can also be helpful. Repetition is good, but remember that our goal is to more than know the verse, it is to live it. **Example: *Our blessing verse to memorize for the Eternity Event is Revelation 7:12 and many songs through the ages have included those words. Play with different tunes and come up with a personalized praise chorus that you can sing out to God at anytime. The "amen" at the beginning and at the end frame up the praiseworthy qualities of God which we love to experience. Visualizing the verse in a different pattern or arrangement can help us too.***

Revelation 7:12
Amen!
Blessing
Glory and Wisdom
Thanksgiving and Honor
Power and Strength
belong to our God
forever and ever!
Amen.
Revelation 7:12

❧

These tips are gathered from my experiences as well as from Nancy Taylor's excellent book: *Taking the Word to Heart*[1], which I highly recommend.

---

[1]Nancy Taylor, Taking the Word to Heart (CrossBooks, 2009)

Deeper Blessings

The following optional ideas are provided to give additional depth to your personal study through God's Story in conjunction with *The Blessing Book Study Guide*. Pick and choose what might be helpful for you in your present situation. There are way more blessings from God and His Word than we will ever be able to fully experience, but go ahead and dive into some **Deeper Blessings**!

༆

✎ If you like to read, then this one might be for you! To go even deeper into the blessings of God's Story, consider looking up the blessing verses from each entry in the study in your own Bible and highlight the "bless" words you read. This means you will be doing a lot of good reading, getting even more familiar with God's Story. We understand better when we get a broader scope of the big picture. As you faithfully incorporate this discipline, His blessings will wonderfully stand out to you in new ways when you reread through your copy of God's Story. Jot down dates, names and situations about which you are praying next to certain blessings to personalize your journey with God even more.

✎ God's Story is a love story. Growing our awareness of love can help us increase our ability to receive and give it appropriately. Underline or draw a heart where love shows up in the entries throughout *The Blessing Book*. **Example: *From the entry on January 2: "As He blessed us, so we should bless the world around us. God is <u>love</u>; it only makes sense that being created in His image means that we were made for <u>love</u> and designed to be <u>loving</u>."***

✎ Go on a blessing hunt. Look for the blessing verses in different translations to get a fuller meaning of the word bless in that specific context. Websites like **BibleGateway.com** can be a big help with this. Jot down what you discover in your Blessing Journal. **Example: *The New King James translation of Psalm***

104:1 reads "Bless the Lord O my soul." In The Voice it is "Call Him good my soul and praise the Eternal..." The "call Him good" helps to define what "bless" means in this context. Another example: When Elizabeth was talking to Mary during their pregnancies, she said, "How fortunate you are, Mary, for you believed that what the Lord told you would be fulfilled." Fortunate is another way to describe blessed. Building a list of how bless is used at different times in different translations expands our understanding of the concept.

🍂 Woven into most of the entries of *The Blessing Book* are opportunities for action. Often these **Action Options** are broad principles. Think through the "how-tos" and prayerfully consider choosing a few actions that you would like to develop further and make them applicable to this season of your life. Knowing God's truth is good. Memorizing it is even better. But where we really want to get is to the place where His truth makes a changing difference in our lives. I have found it takes a while for a desired habit to become a habit in reality. What may help is to try not to take on too many changes all at once, but instead solidify a new habit and then build. Page 68 begins a list of Action Options for you to consider.

Ideas for Using a Blessing Journal

🍂 Consider getting a journal or a notebook to record blessings you have received and blessing that you give. Think about how God has blessed you today. Praise Him for specific ways He has given you provision and protection in your life. Try to record at least one blessing (big or not so big) which you notice each day. God uses His Word, other people, creation, as well as circumstances to draw our attention to Him and to the blessings He gives. As we grow in attentiveness, we will grow in our awareness of His love and also of the opportunities to love those around us.

🍂 Throughout the week think about who or how you can bless and then pray for opportunities to bless. To help make the idea of blessing more concrete, write down a little reminder in your Blessing Journal of your desire to bless. **Example: *I have not seen one of my neighbors in quite some time. So I have written "AG" in my notebook and began to pray for a way to connect with her. Jot down when you have been able to bless, the situation around the blessing,*** *and maybe even how you feel about it. Do some of your feelings include being happy, joyful, blessed? I hope so. There will be other times when God uses you as an instrument of blessing without you even planning to! Jot down these too. Thank Him for finding you trustworthy to share goodness in His Kingdom. Don't lose heart. Like answers to prayer, not all blessings come about in our desired timing. Keep pressing into God with your resolve to bless and seek Him for the details.*

From time to time, reread your Blessing Journal. Doing this can build our awareness of God's faithfulness in our lives. This kind of faith building is crucial when dry times come. As we reflect on His past interactions with us, we have hope that He is with us now in the new unknowns of life and its challenges.

The size of your journal can make a difference. At times when life seemed to be lived on the go I used a smaller notebook that I could carry with me and I was always ready to add to it. Other seasons in life I recorded "blessings" on a normal calendar. Some might find that a pretty journal is inspiring to fill. Choose what is right for you for now. The purpose is to begin the habit of recording interactions of love and goodness that happen to you, and from you, with God and with people.

Be sure to date your blessing entries and notice if any themes emerge. We can discover more of who we are as we give attention to how interacting with God and with people in loving and appropriate ways takes shape. God's plan from the beginning is to bless. Let's intentionally be aware of and part of His plan.

Sometimes sharing your experience of blessing can be an encouragement to you and to others. I like the example of Mary and the wisdom we can learn from her. When the message settled in that she was to be the mother of Jesus, she excitedly told this good news to her cousin Elisabeth. The blessing was doubled as joy was shared. At another time the Bible records that Mary "pondered all these things in her heart" (Luke 2:19). Ecclesiastes 3 teaches us that there is a time and a season for everything. When it comes experiencing specific blessings, I believe that there is a how and a when and a why we share those blessing experiences with others. Pray for wisdom for when to share and for when to treasure in your heart the blessings you experience.

Blessings received or given lead to gratitude. All good gifts come from our Heavenly Father so let's be quick to thank Him. Do not get caught up in seeking a blessing over seeking our Lord. By jotting down little reminders of gratitude we can improve our attitude and increase our happiness potential.

"Bless God from whom all blessings flow.
Bless Him ye creatures here below.
Bless Him above ye Heavenly host.
Bless Father, Son and Holy Ghost.
Amen."

Action Options

God's goodness and grace in our lives leads us to want to honor and bless Him and the best way for a student to honor his or her teacher is to take in and then live out what the teacher teaches. Jesus is the best at teaching and living out love. To be able to love like He does requires us to train in character growth. It is exciting how diligent training can transform conceptual love into the reality of love in action. Life is a process so some of the **Action Options** will be reminders of things you already know and do, and others may capture your attention and affection to become new habits. This list offers you ways to go deeper in your journey in living a life of blessings. The dates below each grouping will help you to find the Action Option in the context of the entries within *The Blessing Book*.

Another good way for the **Action Options** to grow you is to use them as prayer prompters. Here is an example of praying the Action Options from Chapter 1: *God, I love you and I really want to seek Your Presence as I go through this day. Please use me to bless the world around me especially... Help me to reflect on Your goodness even in light of... Keep my mind aware of the way You bless me. Today I'm thankful for... People around the world need to know Your love and goodness, please draw Rain closer to You as she makes choices outside of the detention center...*

•⟩ CHAPTER 1 ⟨•

SEEK God's Presence daily · *BLESS* the world around me · *REFLECT* on God's goodness · *BE* aware of one blessing after another today · *PRAY* for Rain (a girl from Thailand)

JANUARY 1–7

•⟩ CHAPTER 2 ⟨•

THINK of how God loves me · *LIVE* from a grateful heart · *BELIEVE*, obey, be blessed! · *THANK* God for my citizenship in Heaven · *WALK* by faith, trusting God with each step

JANUARY 8–13

MAKE progress on changing according to God's plan · *TRUST* God with the lives of those I love most · *PRAY* for godly marriage partners as it applies to self, children, others · *GO* to God voicing my specific concerns · *PRAY* specifically for God's intervention

JANUARY 14–19

PRAY for those who expand my family tree · *TAKE* heart, God answers prayer · *REFLECT* on my many blessings · *DRAW* near to God in stress filled times · *BE* not afraid

JANUARY 20–24

LOVE without favoritism · *REMEMBER* God's past blessings · *SEEK* God's guidance through confusion · *OFFER* forgiveness · *HOLD* on to hope

JANUARY 25–29

PRAY for committed marriages · *CHOOSE* to walk in step with Jesus · *REFLECT* on my life · *ALLOW* blessings to flow · *BLESS* those I love

JANUARY 30–FEBRUARY 3

WRESTLE with God until there is a break-through · *FORGIVE* one another · *REMEMBER:* God is over this world, He gives hope · *HOLD* on to God who redeems and blesses · *BE* lead by God to bless others

FEBRUARY 4–8

LEAVE a legacy of thanksgiving · *ALLOW* blessings to flow from my heart and lips · *EXTEND* blessings while I can · *LIVE* humbly and joyfully where God places me · *HONOR* God by sharing His goodness

FEBRUARY 9–13

• CHAPTER 3 •

SOFTEN my heart to God's ways · *SEEK* to see from God's perspective · *THANK* and bless God · *OBEY* God; it shows my loyalty · *HONOR* God

FEBRUARY 14–19

WORSHIP God even in tragedy · *INTERCEDE* on behalf of others · *SERVE* God faithfully · *LIVE* out Jesus' teachings · *TALK* to God about my needs

FEBRUARY 20–24

CALL out to God for intervention · *FEEL* the warmth and love of God's smile · *GROW* close to God along my journey · *STAY* near to God even when it feels like my enemy has the upper hand · *FOCUS* on God's Presence

FEBRUARY 25–MARCH 1

THANK God for the blessing of His direction · *REMEMBER:* God is trustworthy · *FOLLOW* God's good laws carefully · *PONDER* God even when I'm filled with blessings · *GIVE* encouragement that instills courage

MARCH 2–6

WALK wholeheartedly in God's ways · *LIVE* joyfully, thankfully, prayerfully *BE* careful to obey; blessings will come · *GIVE* generously, live generously *RETURN* blessing for blessing

MARCH 7–11

TRUST in the simple yet profound truth that God loves me · *LOVE* like God loves · *BE* creative, be generous, be a blessing! · *OBEY* God—it leads to blessings · *REMAIN* faithful to God who cares for me

MARCH 12–16

VALUE God's love and wisdom over all · *GO* forth loving those in a world that is still upside-down · *CHOOSE* life! · *RESPOND* with gratitude to the blessings I'm given · *SPEAK* strongly for my Lord

MARCH 17–21

RUN strong and pass on the baton of faith · *FOLLOW* my Lord wholeheartedly · *EXTEND* blessings · *PRAY* for those who lead · *LOVE* my Lord completely

MARCH 22–26

SERVE and obey my Lord · *USE* the tools that God gives me to faithfully contribute · *PRAISE* God for victories · *UTILIZE* my uniqueness to honor my Lord · *PRAY* for the people of Burma

MARCH 27–31

HAVE faith that God will bless · *LIVE* filled with my Lord's blessing · *REFLECT* on the truth that all goodness comes from God · *REMEMBER:* bitter hearts can change and joy can follow · *LIVE* with eternity in mind

APRIL 1–6

MODEL a spiritual life of thanksgiving · *BE* wise with my requests · *OBEY* God fully, not partially · *STAY* close to God in hard times · *TASTE* and see that my Lord is good

APRIL 7–11

CALL out to God for help · *EXTEND* the peace that God has blessed me with · *WALK* with God · *PRAISE* God from whom all blessings flow · *DO* right because it is right

APRIL 12–16

WORK together in awareness of God · *SEEK* peace · *RETURN* blessings with blessings · *CHOOSE* to live life following God's blueprints · *LIVE* loyally to my Lord

APRIL 17–21

MEDITATE on the glory of God's splendor · *COUNT* my blessings; name them one by one · *SING* out loudly to God · *BLESS* God with a grateful heart · *SEEK* to joyfully meet the needs of others

APRIL 22–26

WAKE up to bless someone each day · *INVEST* in the lives of children · *CELEBRATE* God · *TELL* of God's goodness · *SHARE* my gratitude to God

APRIL 27–MAY 1

DRINK deeply from God's wisdom · *ENTER* into God's shelter · *SHARE* God's goodness · *HOLD* fast to God's blessings while reaching out to bless *FEAST* on Jesus, the Bread of Life

MAY 2–6

CHOSE to be thankful · *BE* in awe of God · *BLESS* my Lord, O my soul *INVEST* wisely in those God has blessed me with · *BE* faithful to bless my Lord

MAY 7–11

RELY on God for my rescue · *CARE* for those who cannot care for themselves *MAKE* extending God's blessings a part of my life · *PRAY* for Hank and his village in Southeast Asia · *SEEK* to bless

MAY 12–16

WALK by faith · *BE* alert and stand firm in my faith · *SHOW* mercy and pray for my enemies · *DO* good, practice generosity, bless others · *LIVE* out healthy spiritual disciplines

MAY 17–21

UNLOAD my anxieties upon my Lord · *BEAR* fruit, dying to self and living for God · *STUDY* diligently · *LEAD* by example to bless my Lord · *TRUST* in God's love and faithfulness

MAY 22–27

⟨ CHAPTER 4 PART 2 ⟩

MAKE a joyful noise unto my Lord · *THANK* Jesus for forgiveness · *PRAY* for London, home to people from almost every nation · *GROW* like the Psalm 1 tree · *KNOW* God; make Him known

MAY 28–JUNE 1

TRUST spiritual insights more than wealth · *HAVE* passion for God · *REIGN* fairly over my sphere of influence · *LIVE* in happy anticipation, waiting for Jesus' return · *SEEK* wisdom and understanding

JUNE 2–7

GET GOOD at making peace · *HEED* wisdom's call · *CHOOSE* to be righteous · *SHARE* with those who are hungry · *LEARN* from my errors

JUNE 8–12

DESIRE peaceful relationships · *REMEMBER* that God will evaluate all things · *LIVE* an upright life · *TREASURE* wisely; put off the bad, put on the good · *PLACE* myself into the Story

JUNE 13–17

CELEBRATE life and live it fully! · *PRAY* for Thai people to have peace with God · *EXALT* God · *SHARE* goodness by blessing my neighbors · *BE* wise

JUNE 18–22

LOVE and obey God · *TAKE* my need for cleansing to Jesus · *KNOW* my true identity in God · *REALIZE* that life is a gift from God · *PRAISE* and thank my Lord

JUNE 23–27

SHARE what I know · *CALL* on God · *LIVE* fully connected to God · *PASS* on good news about God · *FIND* my satisfaction in God

JUNE 28–JULY 2

DRINK in God's teachings · *CONNECT* to the Giver of all things good · *LIVE* loyally to my Lord · *BE* just, merciful and humble · *ALIGN* with God

JULY 3–7

RETURN to my Lord · *OFFER* up the blessing of thanksgiving · *REJOICE* in the rescue God brings! · *KEEP* growing · *THIRST* for God's Word

JULY 8–12

REFLECT on God's goodness · *HONOR* God by treating others with kindness · *GO* forward as a blessing · *PRAY* for those in juvenile detention centers · *SEEK* God and be blessed

JULY 13–17

•〉 CHAPTER 5 〈•

ASK God to lead · *LET* go of the things I value more than God · *BREAK* the cycle of treasuring sin · *SING* with joy, for my confidence is in my Lord · *DO* what is right

JULY 18–23

DEAL with situations in right ways · *RESOLVE* to live presently and thankfully · *MAGNIFY* God's goodness · *CALL* out for God to hear me · *THANK* Jesus for freedom from my shortcomings

JULY 24–28

PRAY for belief and trust in God to come for those I love · *GIVE* back to God while giving forward to people · *HONOR* God joyfully · *LEARN* from Job's integrity during hard times · *BE* wise to contemplate that I am not exempt from suffering

JULY 29–AUGUST 2

REMAIN faithful in times of testing · *KNOW* that Jesus did not come to give me an easy life, but eternal life · *HOLD* tight to Jesus in my pain · *STAY* loyal to God when severe trials come · *HATE* sin but love my enemies

AUGUST 3–8

LIVE a life of hope · *STAND* up for good and for God · *GIVE* careful thought to my ways · *HONOR* God with my body, mind, and actions · *WORK* hard, be truthful, be a peacemaker

AUGUST 9–13

VALUE justice and mercy · *CALL* on the name of my Lord · *LEARN* and apply what God teaches · *GIVE* to God · *TAKE* courage for whatever God puts before me

AUGUST 14–18

PRAY for God's protection · *GROW* close to God with the anticipation of His provision · *UNWRAP* God's gifts of blessings, delight in them, and share them *EXALT* God about all · *TURN* to God

AUGUST 19–22

• CHAPTER 6 •

FOCUS on God's Presence when faced with decisions · *SHARE* good news · *BELIEVE* in the faithfulness of God · *TAKE* great joy in my Savior · *LOVE* those God places in my path

AUGUST 23–27

PRAISE God for rescue, redemption, and redirection · *ALLOW* happy tears to freely fall · *ADORE* Jesus · *BE* amazed with Jesus · *READ* Matthew 5 in a variety of Bible translations

AUGUST 28–SEPTEMBER 1

MOURN when I choose my selfishness over God's goodness · *BE* meek toward God · *HUNGER* and thirst for righteousness · *TAKE* compassion and put it to action · *CHOOSE* to live a pure, non-mixed life

SEPTEMBER 2–6

PLANT seeds of peace · *HOLD* on to hope · *LIVE* out my God created identity · *TAKE* my needs to Jesus · *ADJUST* my understanding of what brings happiness

SEPTEMBER 7–11

LOVE, do good, bless, and pray for those who hurt me · *BE* easy on people · *PRESS* on; God does care · *EXPERIENCE* relief · *LIVE* in blessed obedience

SEPTEMBER 12–16

ALIGN my life with God's teachings • *GO* forward bravely • *OFFER* thanks to God • *SEEK* the Giver of the blessing • *INTERACT* with others in a way that blesses

SEPTEMBER 17–21

PRAY and go and give • *SHARE* the good news: Jesus rescues from death to life! • *LOVE* my neighbor as myself • *SERVE* my Servant-King • *BLESS* people who can not bless me back

SEPTEMBER 22–26

SHARE truth and offer hope • *RUN* to Jesus • *BLESS* Jesus for His steadfast commitment to all that is right • *LIVE* faithfully in times of celebration and trials • *REJOICE* and praise God with a loud voice

SEPTEMBER 27–OCTOBER 1

PRAISE God in highest Heaven • *SERVE* faithfully and sensibly • *CARE* for those who need care • *GET* back on track when I miss the mark of loving God and loving people • *REMEMBER* Jesus: broken for me to have wholeness through Him

OCTOBER 2–6

TRUST Jesus • *TAKE* heart, Jesus overcame the world • *BELIEVE* that Jesus is the blessing • *BELIEVE* by faith • *LIVE* a life to bless God with great joy

OCTOBER 7–11

• > CHAPTER 7 PART 1 < •

TURN to face God • *LIVE* bravely for God • *FOLD* my hands in gratitude and open them up for godly giving • *BE* an encourager • *HOLD* on to the facts

OCTOBER 12–16

LIVE out the blessing of peace • *DESIRE* to both learn and teach • *GIVE* up prideful ways of thinking • *LIVE* as a grateful, free person • *CHOOSE* to bless

OCTOBER 17–21

LIVE life with joy and great hope • *PRESS* on in the strength God provides *GROW* up in the character of Christ • *HELP* the weak • *VALUE* Jesus more than anything else

OCTOBER 22–26

DO my part in expanding God's Kingdom · *BUILD* on the foundation of Jesus · *LIVE* out the story of love and commitment · *EMBRACE* afresh the good news that God loves me · *UNIFY* around Jesus

OCTOBER 27–31

SEEK to connect meaningfully with people of different cultures *COMMUNICATE* in understandable ways · *PRACTICE* hospitality · *OFFER* meaningful comfort to others · *RELY* on God and not my own strength

NOVEMBER 1–5

APPLY truth to my life · *BE* generous · *BOAST* in Jesus · *HEED* Paul's warning to honor God · *BE* free to work, serve, and live in joy

NOVEMBER 6–10

SEEK to achieve God's standard of righteousness by faith · *ACKNOWLEDGE* that God will be blessed forever · *CALL* out for Jesus to rescue me · *EMBRACE* God's grace · *SAY* "yes" to God's invitation to work with Him

NOVEMBER 11–15

BE grafted into God's family · *RESPOND* with sincere kindness · *TAKE* time to think through what I do or do not do · *DEPEND* on God for my relational needs · *FINISH* my course with joy

NOVEMBER 16–20

LIVE for what is right · *OFFER* grace and peace · *DEVELOP* my ability to love God and love people · *PARTICIPATE* in God's blessing · *LIVE* out reconciliation and restoration

NOVEMBER 21–25

GROW in maturity · *SHARE* with others God's plan of adoption · *THINK* about things that are pure, noble and praiseworthy · *BE* an example of peace and forgiveness · *BLESS* as I have been blessed

NOVEMBER 26–30

PRACTICE integrity · *PURSUE* righteousness · *LIVE* a redeemed life *PARTNER* in growing God's love · *BECOME* usable to God and others

DECEMBER 1–5

GAIN a realistic perspective of trials · *STUDY* God's Story and live it out *RID* myself of hypocrisy · *PERSEVERE* · *BE* built up in the faith

DECEMBER 6–10

RECEIVE abundant life and a living hope · *BE* tenderhearted · *KEEP* calm and carry on in the ways that honor God · *ADVANCE* toward transformation · *CHECK* my character growth

DECEMBER 11–15

IMITATE those who live faithfully · *WATER* souls with prayer · *PULL* out by the roots any bitterness · *PRACTICE* discernment · *COMPREHEND* that God offers mercy instead of punishment

DECEMBER 16–21

CHAPTER 8

READ and embrace God's truth · *JOIN* the masses to praise God · *SEE* people as God sees them · *FIND* rest from my labor · *LIVE* expectantly!

DECEMBER 22–26

BELIEVE it: the wedding supper celebration will be blessed! · *KEEP* in mind that I'm part of God's Story · *CONTEMPLATE* God's grace that is beyond amazing · *WORSHIP* God alone · *LIVE* blessed!

DECEMBER 27–31

Made in the USA
Charleston, SC
30 March 2016